WILL ANY GENTLEMAN?

A Farce in Three Acts

by

VERNON SYLVAINE

SAMUEL FRENCH

LONDON
NEW YORK   TORONTO   SYDNEY   HOLLYWOOD

Copyright © 1952 by Vernon Sylvaine
All Rights Reserved

WILL ANY GENTLEMAN? is fully protected under the copyright laws of the British Commonwealth, including Canada, the United States of America, and all other countries of the Copyright Union. All rights, including professional and amateur stage productions, recitation, lecturing, public reading, motion picture, radio broadcasting, television and the rights of translation into foreign languages are strictly reserved.

ISBN 978-0-573-01490-1

www.samuelfrench.co.uk

www.samuelfrench.com

For Amateur Production Enquiries

UNITED KINGDOM AND WORLD EXCLUDING NORTH AMERICA

plays@SamuelFrench-London.co.uk

020 7255 4302/01

Each title is subject to availability from Samuel French,

depending upon country of performance.

CAUTION: Professional and amateur producers are hereby warned that WILL ANY GENTLEMAN? is subject to a licensing fee. Publication of this play does not imply availability for performance. Both amateurs and professionals considering a production are strongly advised to apply to the appropriate agent before starting rehearsals, advertising, or booking a theatre. A licensing fee must be paid whether the title is presented for charity or gain and whether or not admission is charged.

The professional rights in this play are controlled by Samuel French Ltd, 52 Fitzroy Street, London, W1T 5JR

No one shall make any changes in this title for the purpose of production. No part of this book may be reproduced, stored in a retrieval system, or transmitted in any form, by any means, now known or yet to be invented, including mechanical, electronic, photocopying, recording, videotaping, or otherwise, without the prior written permission of the publisher. No one shall upload this title, or part of this title, to any social media websites.

The right of Vernon Sylvaine to be identified as author of this work has been asserted in accordance with Section 77 of the Copyright, Designs and Patents Act 1988.

WILL ANY GENTLEMAN?

Produced at the Strand Theatre, London, W.C.2, on September 6th, 1950, with the following cast of characters:

(in the order of their appearance)

A DANCER	*Patricia Dare*
MENDOZA, a hypnotist	*Norman Scace*
ALBERT BOYLE	*Wilfred Boyle*
ANGEL, Mendoza's assistant	*Thelma Grigg*
HENRY STIRLING	*Robertson Hare*
BERYL, the maid	*Natalie Raine*
DR SMITH	*Charles Groves*
FLORENCE STIRLING, Henry's wife	*Constance Lorne*
CHARLEY STIRLING, Henry's brother	*Arthur Riscoe*
DETECTIVE INSPECTOR MARTIN	*Henry Caine*
STANLEY JACKSON, a bank manager	*Hugh Metcalfe*
HONEY	*Pamela Deeming*
MRS WHITTLE, Florence's mother	*Ruth Maitland*
MONTAGUE BILLING, a director of the bank	*Gerard Clifton*

The Play Produced by RICHARD BIRD

SYNOPSIS OF SCENES

ACT I

SCENE 1. A suburban Music-Hall. About 9 p.m. on a Thursday evening in Summer

SCENE 2. The living-room of HENRY STIRLING's house in Hampstead Garden Suburb. About 5.30 p.m. the following evening

ACT II

SCENE 1. The same. About 10 a.m. the following morning
SCENE 2. The same. Two hours later

ACT III

SCENE 1. A dressing-room at the Music-Hall. About 6.45 p.m. the same day.

SCENE 2. The living-room of HENRY STIRLING's house. About 7.15 p.m. the same day

Throughout the play the abbreviations R. and L. indicate stage right and stage left

WILL ANY GENTLEMAN?

ACT I

SCENE 1

SCENE.—*A Suburban Music-Hall. About 9 p.m. on a Thursday evening in Summer.*
A colourful backcloth hangs about three feet up stage from the footlights. R. *and* L., *on the proscenium arch facing the audience, there are the usual electrically operated frames indicating the number of the turn. There are steps down* R. *and down* L., *leading from the stage to the auditorium. It is important that the steps be built as unobtrusively as possible. They must not look strangely out of place when the Scene is no longer a Music-Hall. For safety, the steps should have a handrail on the proscenium wall side. The set for Scene 2 is already in position except for the downstage* R. *and* L. *flats.*
  At the conclusion of the Overture, the house lights go out, the number frames light up with the number "five" and the music suddenly breaks into music-hall accompaniment for a modern Can-can number. In the darkness, ALBERT BOYLE *and* HENRY STIRLING *enter the auditorium unobtrusively and take their seats.* BOYLE *at the right of the stalls and* HENRY *at the left of a row near the pit. If steps can only be arranged at one side of the stage—either* R. *or* L.*—then* BOYLE *and* HENRY *must both be seated on the same side of the auditorium.* BOYLE, *an undertaker, is tall, thin and lugubrious,* HENRY *is short and timid with a familiar moustache. He carries a bowler hat and an umbrella.*

After a minute or so, the CURTAIN *rises. The* DANCER, *a girl in Can-can dress is nearing the end of her dance. After about half a minute, the dance finishes, the music concludes with the usual music-hall flourish and the* DANCER *exits* L. *as—*
  the CURTAIN *falls.*
  The backcloth is replaced by tabs that look like black velvet and a chair is set L.C. *The number frames change to the number "six". There is a bugle fanfare.*

When the CURTAIN *rises, the stage is empty. The fanfare ceases and* MENDOZA *enters through the centre divide of the tabs. As he does so, he is picked up by a spotlight which follows him in the usual music-hall fashion as he moves about the stage. He is a Rasputin type of individual, pale, long-haired, oily, crafty, slick, furtive and frightening. On occasions he employs a tremendously forceful manner, but his whispers are equally ominous. He wears a shabby frock coat with a tucked-in black scarf in place of collar and tie; his hands are long and white and he knows how to use them. In speech, gesture and manner he is Continental plus. He moves down* c. *and addresses the audience in a heavy Austrian-type accent. In music-hall fashion he seldom looks away from the audience and frequently addresses his remarks to the gallery.*

MENDOZA. Ledies und gentlemen, it is wiz moch plaisure zat I introduce myself to you at zis music-'all zis evenings. Plis, I ask you not to make merriment against me because I not spik British very goot. My name is Paul Gerhart Mendoza. I am a zychological 'ipnotist. Ah! No smilings! Vait und see. I 'ave spent twenty years of my life wiz ye mysteries of Oriental mesmerism. I know, of course, zat zere are sighnical people 'oo do not believe in mystic power. For zem, I can only repetition—vait und see. Und now—vill any gentleman kom to me on ze stage? Plis. Vill any gentleman?

(ALBERT BOYLE *rises from his seat in the stalls.*)

(*To* BOYLE.) Sank you, sir. Zat vos very quick.

(BOYLE *ascends to the stage and stands* L.C. *He carries his programme.*)

Sometimes I 'ave moch trouble to persvade somebody. Sank you very mooch. Zis vay, plis. (*He moves to* R. *of* BOYLE *and shakes hands with him.*) I 'ave moch plaisure wiz meeting you. Vot is your name?
   BOYLE (*quietly*). Albert Boyle.
   MENDOZA. Speak up! Sink of ze audience.
   BOYLE (*loudly*). Albert Boyle.
   MENDOZA (*to the audience*). Oh! Zat is depressing. (*To* BOYLE.) I sink you should forget a name like zat.
   BOYLE. How *can* I?
   MENDOZA (*smiling and quietly*). You are *going* to.
   BOYLE. Oh no, I'm not.
   MENDOZA. Oh yes, you are. You vill even forget zat you 'ave bin to zis music 'all. Look at me. Look at my eyes.

(BOYLE *looks at* MENDOZA.)

(*He stretches out his hands towards* BOYLE. *Intensely.*) Already you are forgetting your name. You are forgetting—you are forgetting—you are forgetting—you 'ave forgotten. (*Suddenly and loudly.*) Vot *is* your name? Vot is your *name?*
   BOYLE (*staring at* MENDOZA). Er—er . . .
   MENDOZA (*indicating the chair* L.C.). Sit down.

(BOYLE, *bewildered, sits on the chair* L.C.)

Vy do you look so miserable?
   BOYLE (*unhappily*). I really *have* forgotten what my name *is.*
   MENDOZA. Zat is nussing to be sad about. Look at me.

(BOYLE *looks at* MENDOZA.)

You are a very 'appy man, do you 'ear? (*Slowly.*) You are so 'appy—you laugh nearly all ze time. Laugh. Laugh.

(BOYLE *gives a hollow lugubrious laugh.*)

(*He laughs then turns to the audience.*) Don't worry, before he leaves the stage I vill bring him safely back to all the unhappiness of complete consciousness. Ledies und gentlemen, I cannot sufficiently stress ze importance zat nobody leave me wizout first being returned to normal condition. On van occasion I tell a gentleman zat 'e is ze eight-twenty train to Brighton. (*He imitates a train.*) He puff puff puff all round und make ze people laugh very moch. But I forget all about 'im—und 'e leave ze stage. On 'is way 'ome 'e arrive at Victoria—und, still sinking 'e is ze eight-twenty to Brighton, 'e gets down on to ze railway line. (*He imitates a train.*) Puff, puff, puff, puff—(*he closes his eyes*) 'e meets ze six-sirty-fife from Eastbourne. Ho, ho, ho! Zere vos moch trouble.

(ANGEL *enters* R. *The spotlight moves from* MENDOZA *to* ANGEL. *She is aged about twenty-six and very attractive. She wears a black velvet evening dress. Her own short dark hair is covered by a dressy black wig.*)

Ah! My Angel. (*To the audience.*) She is so sveet. (*He rubs his hands together. Happily.*) Ve 'ave such friendships. No, sir, not vot *you* sink. (*Solemnly.*) I am 'er guardian.

(BOYLE *laughs. The spotlight moves to* MENDOZA.)

(*To the audience. Briskly.*) Und now! Vill any gentleman 'oo is shy kom to me on ze stage? Very particular, I vish for somebody 'oo is shy.

ANGEL (*to the audience*). Will any gentleman?

(*If any over-confident member of the audience makes a move,* MENDOZA *refuses him on the ground that, obviously, he is not shy.*)

MENDOZA. I will not do anysing bad to 'im—zat I promise on my word of honour.

(BOYLE *laughs.*)

I sink per'aps Angel vill know 'oo is most suitable. (*To* ANGEL.) Plis, my darling—find for me a shy man.

(*The auditorium lights go up.* ANGEL *smilingly descends to the auditorium.* BOYLE *rises and tries to walk in to the wings* L.)

(*He crosses to* BOYLE.) Hey! Vere are you going? Ve 'ave not finished wiz you yet.

(BOYLE *whispers to* MENDOZA.)

No, you must vait. (*He moves* C.)

(BOYLE *sits on the chair* L.C. ANGEL *smilingly moves up the side of the stalls. If any member of the audience volunteers, she refuses him, because, obviously, he isn't shy.*)

(*To the audience.*) I must ask zat no vun gets—'ow you say—fresh wiz my Angel. She is a goot girl—only seventeen years of age.

(BOYLE *gives a lugubrious laugh.* MENDOZA *glares at him. Suddenly, from somewhere near the pit, there is a panic-stricken shout.*)

HENRY. No, please!
MENDOZA. Ah! Vot 'ave ve found?
HENRY. No! I don't want to.

(ANGEL *drags* HENRY *down towards the front of the auditorium. He clutches his bowler hat and umbrella.*)

MENDOZA. Yes. Angel 'as got somesing. Zis way. Do not struggle. Nussing vill 'appen to you. Anysing broken, I mend it.
HENRY (*on his unwilling way*). No. You've no right to do this. Leave me alone. I'll take no part in it. Please!
MENDOZA. Such protests. Vot is ze matter wiz 'im?

(*The laughing* ANGEL *pulls* HENRY *on to the stage, stands him* R.C., *then moves* R. *The auditorium lights go out.*)

(*To* HENRY.) I am not going to 'urt you. Zere is no need to be frightened.

(HENRY *suddenly turns and tries to return to the auditorium.* ANGEL *stops him.*)

(*He moves to* L. *of* HENRY *and takes the bowler hat and umbrella from him.*) Ah! No running avay.

(*The spotlight now concentrates on* HENRY.)

HENRY (*loudly, towards the wings*). Where's the manager?
MENDOZA. Vy do you vant to disturb 'im?
HENRY (*to* MENDOZA; *angrily*). Give me my umbrella.
MENDOZA. Vy? It is not raining. (*He moves to* BOYLE, *places* HENRY's *hat on* BOYLE's *head and hands him the umbrella.*) 'Ere, stupid vun—look after zem for ze gentleman. (*He turns to* HENRY. *With a smile.*) Zere now—you are not still cross wiz my Angel?
HENRY. I'm not interested in your female friends. I dislike this sort of thing intensely.
MENDOZA (*moving* C.). You 'ave no respect for my vork?
HENRY. No, I have not.
MENDOZA. Oh, you are septical, huh? You do not sink I can 'ave power over you?
HENRY (*angrily*). I think you're an impertinent mountebank.

(ANGEL *forces a laugh towards the audience.*)

MENDOZA. So! Now ve 'ave insults, huh? (*Angrily.*) Vy do you

kom to such a place if you are so 'igh and mighty?
HENRY. I didn't really mean to come here at all.
MENDOZA (*to the audience*). You know somesing? I am a great student of 'uman nature. I sink 'e is not telling me ze troos. (*To* HENRY.) Vot is your name?
HENRY. Mind your own business.
MENDOZA (*to the audience*). Vy does 'e seem so uneasy—so vurried und so guilty? Ha, ha! Zere is somsing ze matter somevere. I smell mice. (*To* HENRY.) Is it zat your vife does not *know* you are at a music-'all?
HENRY. Ridiculous!
MENDOZA. Look at me.
HENRY. I will not.

(*There is a moment's pause, then* HENRY *slowly turns a worried face to* MENDOZA.)

MENDOZA (*staring hard at* HENRY). Per'aps you sink my eyes are getting bigger, huh? Per'aps you are feeling confused and dizzy. Even per'aps you are vundering if, after all, ze mountebank 'as some power wiz you. Und 'ow right you vould be. Listen, my little 'igh 'at frient—listen to vot I say. (*Slowly.*) Everysing I ask you—you vill tell me ze troos—you onderstand?
HENRY (*feebly*). Yes, sir.

(*When asking the following six questions, although addressing his remarks to* HENRY, MENDOZA *looks and smiles at the audience.*)

MENDOZA. Vot is your name?
HENRY. Henry.
MENDOZA. Henry—vot else?
HENRY (*pleadingly*). No.
MENDOZA. You do not like to tell me?
HENRY. No.
MENDOZA. Vy not?
HENRY. I don't want anybody to know I'm here.
MENDOZA (*smiling*). Und vy do you not vant zat?
HENRY (*feebly*). My wife thinks I'm at a Rotary meeting.
MENDOZA (*to* HENRY). Und vy are you *not* at ze Rotary meetings?
HENRY. I couldn't stand the old routine any longer. I felt I wanted to kick over the traces.
MENDOZA (*to* HENRY). I onderstand. (*To the audience.*) It is anuzzer form of middle-age spread. Ze years are passing. It is later zan we sink. Hey-ho! Let us 'ave a good bang and go to ze music-'all.
HENRY. Exactly.
MENDOZA (*looking at* HENRY). But you do not vant people to know you feel like zat?
HENRY. Good heavens, no! Please don't tell anybody.

(BOYLE *laughs lugubriously.*)

MENDOZA. You are afraid for your respectabilities, is zat it?
HENRY. Yes.
MENDOZA (*to the audience*). Joost a little respectable citizen—'oo vorks 'ard—pays 'is income tax—kisses 'is vife on ze cheek—und never looks at anuzzer voman.
HENRY. That's right.
MENDOZA (*to the audience*). You know somsing? I sink zere is *anuzzer* side of 'im.
HENRY. There could be—if I didn't control it.
MENDOZA (*to* HENRY). Ah! (*To the audience.*) You know vot is ze matter? He 'as got vot Dr Liebre used to call ze "Dobble Ich". Ze two persons in vun. Ze two complete different personalities. Vun, ze ev'ry-day little man 'oo is so goot—and ze uzzer, ho, ho, ho! (*To* HENRY.) Ze Casanova, huh?
HENRY (*folding his arms*). Maybe.
MENDOZA (*to the audience*). I vunder vot vould 'appen if I remove *all* ze inhibitions. Vot if I release zat *uzzer* personality? Oh, don't vurry. I cannot make 'im vot 'e is not. (*He turns to* HENRY. *Ominously.*) But I *can* bring to ze surface vot 'e already is—deep down insite. Vot 'e 'as always *vanted* to be. *Zat* I can do—because zat is *him*. (*Without looking away from* HENRY, *he raises his hand and calls.*) Cut ze lights.

(*All the stage lighting is blacked out except for one spotlight on* HENRY.)

(*He moves to* L. *of* HENRY, *places his right hand at the back of* HENRY'S *head, his left hand under* HENRY'S *chin, and stares into his eyes. Slowly; with much emphasis.*) Are you listening, Mr 'Enry? (*In a loud whisper.*) Let yourself go.

(*A soft weird noise, like that of a saw-violin is heard.*)

(*He gently strokes* HENRY'S *forehead and stares into his eyes.*) 'Ow you feel now, eh? Like you 'ave 'ad many bottles of champagne, eh? No longer ze little fellow. Now you are ze big shot. Plenty of money—und vine, vomen und song. Ze 'ot-stuff man about town. Zat is 'ow you vould 'ave *like* to be, huh?
HENRY. Yes.
MENDOZA. Splendid. (*He releases* HENRY *and calls.*) Lights, plis. (*Apparently exhausted, he wipes his own forehead.*)

(*The stage lights come up.* HENRY *turns and smiles wickedly at* ANGEL.)

Oh! So soon. Vot you sink of her?
HENRY. I think she's smashing.
MENDOZA. You vould like to kiss 'er?
HENRY. I wanted to kiss her when she first came on to the stage.
MENDOZA (*to the audience*). Zat is becos—since 'e vos a young man—'e 'ave never kiss ze vomen 'e vanted to kiss.
HENRY (*to* ANGEL; *smiling*). I think you're the loveliest thing I've ever seen. I feel I've known you all my life.

MENDOZA. Ha, ha, ha! Now 'e is remembering ze first little girl 'e meet at school.

(HENRY *moves to* L. *of* ANGEL *and kisses her left cheek.*)

(*To the audience.*) Zat is vy 'e kisses 'er on ze cheek. So nice.

(HENRY *suddenly takes* ANGEL *in his arms and kisses her well and truly on her mouth.*)

(*To the audience.*) I don't know 'oo 'e is remembering now. I don't sink it is 'is vife.

(HENRY *releases* ANGEL *and turns to* MENDOZA.)

HENRY (*loudly*). Would you mind going away, please? I wish to be alone with Angel.

(BOYLE *laughs lugubriously.* MENDOZA *rocks with laughter.*)

(*To* ANGEL. *Angrily.*) Excuse me, my dear—there's only one way to deal with a fellow like this. (*He removes his jacket, drops it on the stage and turns up a cuff.*)

(ANGEL *laughs happily towards the audience, but at the same time she places a restraining hand on* HENRY'S *arm and whispers an urgent aside.*)

ANGEL. Stop it! Don't be a fool!

MENDOZA (*to* HENRY). Hey, hey, hey! Plis to remember zat you are in front of ze British public.

HENRY (*livid*). Are you dictating to *me*? We don't stand for dictators in this country, sir. (*To* ANGEL.) Let me go! I'll thrash the hide off him. (*He manages to free one arm and takes a mighty swipe at* MENDOZA.)

MENDOZA (*tottering back and collapsing on top of* BOYLE). No! 'Elp! Stop 'im!

ANGEL (*calling off up* L.). Harry! Curtain! Quickly! Blackout!

ANGEL *screams and holds* HENRY, MENDOZA *shouts, and* BOYLE *laughs as—*
the CURTAIN *quickly falls*

SCENE 2

SCENE.—*The living-room of* HENRY STIRLING'S *house in Hampstead Garden Suburb. About 5.30 p.m. the following day.*

It is a pleasant colourful room. There is a bay window with a built-in window seat R., *overlooking the garden. The fireplace is* L. *Up* L.C. *there is a recess showing the bottom four stairs of the staircase that runs up and off* L. *Up* R.C., *there is an arch leading to the hall, the front door, and the kitchen. There is a small window in the* R. *wall of the hall. The set is built on a slight slant, with the archway a trifle more up stage* than the recess of the stairway. A door up L. leads to another small room. There is a comfortable armchair down R. and a sofa to match, L.C. A small table with a drawer stands in the bay window. There is a dining table R.C., with chairs L. of it, R. of it, and above it. A small table with a telephone on it stands up C. The hall is furnished with a grandfather clock above the window R., a cabinet with a vase of flowers against the wall, an ornate hanging lantern and a picture or two on the walls. In the recess there is a tall stand with a large palm, a dining chair and pictures on the back wall. In the room, above and below the bay window, there are built-in bookshelves, well filled with books. There is also a small set of shelves built into the wall below the fireplace, the shelves being filled with decorative china. Below these shelves, there is a small table set with a decanter and some glasses. Another small table stands below the stairs. As it is summer, there is no fire and an ornamental firescreen stands in the hearth. The room is fitted with a colourful carpet and at night is lit by a standard lamp up R. and two pairs of electric-candle wall-brackets over the mantelpiece.

(*See the Ground Plan and Photograph of the Scene.*)

When the CURTAIN *rises*, DR SMITH *is standing up* C., *speaking into the telephone. He is elderly, frail, charming, and lovable. His stethoscope hangs around his neck. His medical bag is on the table* R.C.

DOCTOR (*into the telephone*). Hullo? Is that Mrs Humday . . . ? Oh, splendid. Er—this is Doctor Smith speaking . . . I'm sorry to trouble you, dear lady, but I'm wondering if I left my stethoscope with you . . . I distinctly remember putting it on your chest but I can't remember where I put it afterwards . . . Mm? . . . Oh . . . Oh, well, I must have put it somewhere else . . . Thank you so much . . . (*He replaces the receiver, and moves towards the table* R.C.) Good-bye. (*He opens his case, peers inside it, looks around him, taps his pockets, glances under the table and suddenly realizes that the stethoscope is hanging round his neck. He gives a little chuckle, removes the stethoscope and places it on the table.*)

(*As he does so,* BERYL, *the maid, enters and comes hurriedly down the stairs. She is aged about thirty-two and is plump and fussy. She is romantic and highly neurotic. Anything out of the ordinary excites her tremendously. There have been no men in her life except for her imaginations in the cinema, but in a forlorn sort of way she might be attractive to the wrong type of elderly man. She wears a black dress and maid's cap and apron. Her character must be taken seriously. She is a human being; not a caricature.*)

BERYL (*as she descends the stairs; excitedly*). Mrs Stirling will be with you in a moment, sir.
DOCTOR. Ah, splendid. How is she?
BERYL (*moving* C.). Oh, there's nothing much wrong with *her*, sir, it's *Mr* Stirling who isn't quite *comme il faut*.

DOCTOR. Yes, yes, of course. What seems to be the trouble?
BERYL. Well, it's nothing physical, sir—not *your* sort of physical—I mean, he doesn't require medicine out of a bottle or anything like that. I don't think there's anything *you* can do for him.
DOCTOR. He's not dead, is he?
BERYL. Oh, no, sir! He's full of life. I've never seen him with such *joie de vivre*.
DOCTOR (*crossing* BERYL *to* L.C.). Then why did Mrs Stirling send for *me?* I was given to understand she was quite hysterical.
BERYL (*smiling coyly*). Ah, that would have been just after it happened.
DOCTOR (*turning*). After *what* happened?
BERYL (*longing to tell*). Well, I don't really know that I ought to mention it, sir.
DOCTOR. Nonsense, girl! I'm a doctor, and if it's anything to do with Mr Stirling's health . . .
BERYL. Oh, I don't think it's anything to do with his health—except, of course, in a roundabout way.
DOCTOR. For heaven's sake, either tell me what happened or stop blithering!
BERYL. Well, this morning—at exactly seven thirty-five a.m.—Mr Stirling pinched my seat.
DOCTOR (*after a moment's reaction*). Do you mean he stole your chair?
BERYL. No, Doctor. It was nothing to do with sitting down—except, of course, in a roundabout way. (*Excitedly*.) I was standing by Mr Stirling's bed—and I had just handed him his early cup of tea and morning paper. Suddenly he dropped the paper—intentionally or otherwise is not for me to say. I bent down to pick it up—and he gave a saucy whistle. Then before I could straighten myself or say "Jack Robinson" . . .
DOCTOR (*interrupting*). Are you actually suggesting that Mr Stirling deliberately assaulted you?
BERYL. Oh, no. There was nothing crude about it. It certainly took me by surprise, but it was all above board. Naturally I gave a little scream—and Mrs Stirling came hurrying from the bathroom to know what had happened. It was no good trying to lie about it. There was Mr Stirling looking ever so guilty—and there was I blushing like an over-ripe apple.
DOCTOR. Tch! Here I am, an extremely busy man, urgently sent for to unravel some kindergarten nonsense to do with pinching bottoms. (*He moves* L.)

(MRS FLORENCE STIRLING *enters and comes down the stairs. She is a slight woman aged about forty-two. She clutches a handkerchief.*)

FLORENCE (*as she enters*). Good afternoon, Doctor.
DOCTOR (*turning*). Eh? Oh. Who's this?

BERYL (*moving* R.C.). This is *Mrs* Stirling, sir. It's she who has been upset by the incident—not me.

FLORENCE (*moving into the room from the stairs; abruptly*). That will do, Beryl. You can get back to the kitchen.

BERYL. No, thank you, madam—(*as she walks to the archway*) I'll retire to my bedroom. (*Looking back.*) I don't *feel* like the kitchen this evening.

(*And with head held proudly high she exits through the archway.*)

FLORENCE. Oh! Impossible!

DOCTOR (*taking a notebook from his pocket and crossing to* R.C.). Mrs Stirling, do forgive me if I ask you to come to the point as quickly as possible. (*He glances at his notebook.*) I still have two carbuncles, one appendix and an evening meal—all to attend to before seven p.m.

FLORENCE (*sitting on the sofa*). Yes, of course.

DOCTOR (*cheerfully*). I don't think I've had the pleasure of meeting you before.

FLORENCE. No. I phoned Dr Morgan, but the secretary said he was away.

DOCTOR (*sitting on the chair* L. *of the table* R.C.). That's right. I'm his locum. Actually, I had retired—oh, many years ago—but so much illness these days and such a shortage of doctors, I'm just giving a helping hand wherever I can. Much too old for the job, of course—one can't help making a slip now and then. I've been working with a broken thermometer for over three days. One of my patients must have bitten it—there's a whole lot of quicksilver *somewhere*—I only hope it's not inside Mrs Humday—she hates anything unusual.

(*Soft orchestral music, played on a gramophone is heard coming from* L. *of the arch up* R.C.)

(*He looks worried, glances towards the window, looks at* FLORENCE, *wiggles his ears with his fingers then looks solemnly and fearfully towards the ceiling.*) Do you hear music?

FLORENCE. Yes.

DOCTOR. Thank God! (*He relaxes and beams happily.*)

FLORENCE. That's the maid again. (*She rises and walks up to the arch.*) She has a gramophone in her bedroom—she's been playing romantic nonsense ever since nine o'clock this morning. (*She calls off through the arch.*) Beryl. Stop that.

(*The music ceases abruptly.*)

DOCTOR. I found her rather strange. No intelligence, of course, and an extremely dull sort of face—and yet now and then, while she was talking to me about a certain incident, she looked positively beautiful.

FLORENCE (*crossing and sitting on the sofa*). She knows nothing about men, Doctor—except what she reads, and she reads too much. She lets her imagination run away with her.

DOCTOR (*rising and crossing to* R. *of* FLORENCE; *cheerfully*). Well, well, we needn't bother about her. It's you we've got to look after at the moment. (*He takes his watch from his pocket, and holds* FLORENCE'S *right wrist and checks her pulse.*) What seems to be the trouble, eh?

FLORENCE (*withdrawing her hand*). It's not me, Doctor. It's my husband. Yesterday was his fiftieth birthday . . .

DOCTOR (*replacing his watch in his pocket*). Ah! That dangerous milestone. Go ahead, dear lady, I'm prepared for anything.

FLORENCE. In the evening, when he came home from the bank . . .

DOCTOR. He *works* in a bank?

FLORENCE. Yes. He's head cashier.

DOCTOR. Splendid!

FLORENCE. He said he was going to a Rotary meeting. I remember thinking he seemed uneasy and restless, but I didn't say anything—and at eight-twenty—he went out.

DOCTOR. But he came home again?

FLORENCE. Yes. At nine-twenty-five.

DOCTOR. Good for him.

FLORENCE. He came home without his hat—without his umbrella—without his jacket—and with lipstick smudged all over his lips.

DOCTOR (*crossing to the fireplace*). Good heavens! I've heard of an umbrella being left behind—but never a complete outfit. (*He turns.*) Did he offer any explanation?

FLORENCE. No. When I started to question him—he told me to go away and leave him alone. I asked him if he would like some cocoa, and he said, "To hell with cocoa! I want some whisky".

DOCTOR. And did he *have* a whisky?

FLORENCE. Yes. Two large ones. He drank them straight off—neat. I've never known him touch alcohol before.

DOCTOR. And what happened then?

FLORENCE. He went to sleep.

DOCTOR (*chuckling*). Well, that was quite understandable.

FLORENCE (*rising*). It wasn't. He went to sleep standing up.

DOCTOR. Do you mean—without support?

FLORENCE. Yes. He stood bolt upright, just in front of the archway there. I thought he might be in a draught so I moved him to in front of the fireplace. It was like moving a statue.

DOCTOR. And how long did he remain like that?

FLORENCE. For at least five minutes. Then I whispered something about it being better if he went to bed—and he smiled and made a clicking noise.

DOCTOR. A clicking noise?

FLORENCE. Yes. (*She makes a clicking noise.*) Like that.

DOCTOR. Ah, yes! I know what that means.

FLORENCE. I did eventually manage to get him upstairs, but I could only half undress him. I was so worried that he might get up in the night and start drinking again—I came downstairs, poured the whisky into a bottle, and filled the decanter up with tea.

DOCTOR (*turning to the table down* L.). Is this it?

FLORENCE. Yes.

DOCTOR (*picking up the decanter*). Cold tea, eh? That wouldn't fool *me*. (*He replaces the decanter.*) And what happened when you went upstairs again, mm?

FLORENCE. He opened his eyes, smiled and said, "Hullo, Angel".

DOCTOR. Ah! He'd realized what a sweet wife he had.

FLORENCE (*tearfully*). No, Doctor. (*She crosses to* R.C.) Angel was the woman with the lipstick.

DOCTOR. Oh dear, oh dear! I'm afraid we must reconcile ourselves to the fact that Mr Stirling has been throwing something of a loose leg. It does happen sometimes, you know—even at fifty. I always think there's something rather sad about it. (*He crosses to* L. *of* FLORENCE.) How was he this morning? Overwhelmed with remorse, I suppose.

FLORENCE. No. He woke up singing. I left him, for a few moments, to turn on his bath . . .

DOCTOR (*crossing* FLORENCE *to* R.). Ah, yes. I know what happened then. He was continental with the maid.

(*Florence closes her eyes.*)

FLORENCE. I came downstairs to see to his breakfast—and when I went up again he'd shaved off his moustache.

DOCTOR. Well, that was nothing very serious.

FLORENCE. I married him with it—(*as she crosses slowly to the sofa; tearfully*) almost *because* of it.

DOCTOR. Well, I dare say it's still somewhere about. How did he appear at breakfast? Did he seem keen to get to his work?

FLORENCE (*sitting on the sofa*). No, he wanted to go to Brighton and stay for the races tomorrow.

DOCTOR. Oh, dear! (*He crosses to* L. *of the table* R.C.) This gambling craze. It's permeating everything. (*He sits* L. *of the table taking his fountain pen from his pocket.*) I suppose he didn't happen to mention any particular horse?

FLORENCE. No.

DOCTOR (*replacing his pen*). Oh.

FLORENCE. I managed to persuade him to think of his duty—and he left for the bank. And *as* he left, he kissed me on the lips.

DOCTOR. Where does he kiss you as a rule?

FLORENCE. On the cheek.

DOCTOR (*rising*). I must look that up.

FLORENCE. Then, at eleven-thirty, the manager phoned to ask

me what was the matter with him. He'd fallen asleep in the wash-room.

DOCTOR. Not standing up?

FLORENCE. Yes.

DOCTOR. Good heavens! (*He moves* C.) I'd better have a look at him. What time does he get home?

FLORENCE (*rising and crossing* R. *below the table*). He should have been here half an hour ago. (*Frantically.*) What can he be doing? Where is he?

DOCTOR (*moving to* L. *of* FLORENCE). Steady, dear lady. The surest way to lose a husband is to keep wondering where you can find him.

FLORENCE. Please do something for him, Doctor.

DOCTOR. I'll do what I can. Although, of course, never having met your husband, I'll be working very much in the dark. Still ...

(*The front-door bell rings off stage.*)

FLORENCE. Here he is.

DOCTOR. I think it will be better if he doesn't *know* I'm Dr Morgan's locum. We don't want to frighten him. (*He leads* FLORENCE *to* C.) You pop upstairs. He'll be safe enough in *my* hands.

FLORENCE. Oh, thank you.

DOCTOR. Ssh! Quickly.

(*Voices are heard off stage.* FLORENCE *exits hurriedly up the stairs. The* DOCTOR *crosses and exits hurriedly* L. *and closes the door behind him.* CHARLEY STIRLING *enters through the archway. He is followed by* BERYL. CHARLEY *is two years younger than his brother* HENRY. *He is a sporty looking fellow who takes nothing very seriously. He carries his hat, a well-rolled umbrella, a small suitcase and a big bunch of summer flowers. He moves* C., *glances around, then turns to* BERYL *and holds out the flowers.*)

CHARLEY (*whispering*). You'd better put these in water.

BERYL (*moving to* R. *of* CHARLEY; *whispering*). Very good, sir. (*She takes the flowers.*) *Who* did you say you were, sir?

CHARLEY (*standing the suitcase beside him on the floor; whispering*). Mr Stirling's brother.

BERYL (*whispering*). Oh. You're not very like him, are you, sir?

CHARLEY (*whispering*). I don't know. I haven't seen him for over five years. (*He hands his hat and umbrella to* BERYL. *In a whisper.*) You'd better put my suitcase in the hall. I don't want to stay if he pegs out.

BERYL (*picking up the suitcase; whispering*). If *who* pegs out, sir?

CHARLEY (*whispering*). My brother, of course. How is he?

BERYL (*whispering*). I've never known him better, sir.

CHARLEY (*whispering*). But he said he was ill.

BERYL (*whispering*). Oh, no, sir. He went out at nine o'clock this morning.

CHARLEY (*angrily and loudly*). Then what the hell are you whispering for?

BERYL (*frightened; loudly*). I don't know, sir. You started it.

CHARLEY (*in his normal voice*). Well, I thought he was upstairs somewhere, dying. He phoned me at half past one—said he was breaking up completely, and begged me to come round and look after him.

BERYL (*in her normal voice; smiling*). Yes, sir, I suppose he *does* need looking after—in a roundabout way—but I think I could manage that better than anybody, if only his wife would let me. (*She suddenly becomes tremendously coy and embarrassed.*) Oh! What am I saying?

(*With an hysterical little laugh, she turns and exits hurriedly through the archway.* CHARLEY *looks mystified, glances around, sees the decanter, smiles, rubs his hands briskly together and crosses to the table down* L.)

CHARLEY (*pouring himself a treble from the decanter and gaily singing*). "Here's to good old whisky, drink it down, drink it down". (*He crosses, sits* L. *of the table* R.C., *raises his glass, beams at the contents and swallows a good half. He immediately bangs down the glass on the table, and his face distorts.*)

(*The* DOCTOR *enters quietly up* L. *and closes the door behind him. He does not see the glass and looks with frightening suspicion at* CHARLEY, *who grimaces terribly, shudders violently and makes loud smacking tasting noises. This business continues reasonably ad lib.*)

DOCTOR (*eventually; moving* C.). Er—are you Mr Stirling?

CHARLEY (*blearing at the* DOCTOR). Well, I *was*—I don't know *who* I am now.

DOCTOR (*hopelessly*). Oh, dear!

CHARLEY (*blearing at the* DOCTOR). Somebody's tried to poison me.

DOCTOR (*soothingly*). Yes, yes, of course. But it'll all pass away.

CHARLEY. I hope so! (*Suddenly.*) Who are *you?*

DOCTOR. I'm an old friend of Mrs Stirling's. A very, very old friend.

CHARLEY. Yes, I can see that.

DOCTOR (*indicating the sofa; with a smile*). Do you mind if I sit down for a moment?

CHARLEY. Not a bit. Sit down—lie down—take your boots off.

DOCTOR. Thank you. (*He sits on the sofa.*) A charming district, Hampstead Garden Suburb.

CHARLEY. I don't know anything about it. I live at Richmond.

DOCTOR (*soothingly*). Yes, yes, of course. And how are you feeling now, mm?

CHARLEY. Terrible.

DOCTOR. Well, you brought it on yourself, you know. (*He chuckles and leans forward towards* CHARLEY.) Fun and games last night, eh?

CHARLEY (*after a pause; very surprised*). Who told *you?*
DOCTOR (*beaming*). A little bird.
CHARLEY (*irritated*). Ah, that's the trouble with Blossom. She will open her mouth.
DOCTOR (*puzzled*). I thought her name was Angel.
CHARLEY. I don't think we're on the same wave-length.
DOCTOR (*briskly*). Ah, well, it doesn't matter. As long as you know where you put your umbrella.
CHARLEY (*after a pause; bewildered*). What are you talking about? I didn't take my umbrella.
DOCTOR. Oh yes, you did.
CHARLEY (*irritated*). Damn it, I ought to know.
DOCTOR (*rising; soothingly*). All right, all right. Don't distress yourself. Let's discuss the matter quite calmly. (*He moves to* L. *of* CHARLEY.) But don't hide things from me, Mr Stirling. I'm a man of the world. Without doubt, the loss of your umbrella has some psychological significance. Quite possibly it's an echo from that far off day when you finally threw aside the shelter and protection afforded you by a fond and loving mother. Oh, I know what I'm talking about. I'm afraid my mother was something of a *Dear Octopus.*
CHARLEY. Is that so? I bet there was something fishy about your *father.*
DOCTOR. Oh, undoubtedly. There's a little of *Oedipus* in all of us.
CHARLEY. He must have got around quite a bit.
DOCTOR (*crossing above the table* R.C. *to* R. *of it; briskly and cheerfully*). Still, we don't need to pursue *him*, do we?
CHARLEY (*turning to face the* DOCTOR). Well, *I'm* not going to bother. It's too late now.
DOCTOR (*taking his watch from his pocket*). Yes, yes, it certainly is. (*He glances at his watch.*) Good heavens! My carbuncles will have to wait until tomorrow. One of them is at Swiss Cottage and the other's at Victoria. It does make things so difficult.

(CHARLEY'S *eyes begin to cross and he rises, moves* C., *and does the crazy business of trying to catch his own finger.*)

(*He watches* CHARLEY *suspiciously for a few moments then moves down* R.) So you went to the bank this morning after all, eh?
CHARLEY (*turning*). Yes, as a matter of fact, I did. It wasn't much good—but I went.
DOCTOR. But you didn't *enjoy* going, did you?
CHARLEY. No. I never do.
DOCTOR. Oh. Why not?
CHARLEY. Well, I always feel so guilty. I mean, the average man just walks into the bank, shouts, "Hiya, Fred!"—that's to the manager—wallops a cheque on to the counter, picks up a bundle of notes in exchange, shouts, "Cheerio-ho, Fred!" and marches out, whistling.

DOCTOR. And what do *you* do?

CHARLEY. Well, first of all I have a good look round. That's before *entering* the bank. Then I turn my collar up and sort of sidle in. Like this. (*As he continues he suits actions to the words.*) Then, if there's nobody about—(*he moves to the back of the sofa*) I edge up to the counter, slide my cheque on to it, and look in the opposite direction. If anything *does* come forth from the kitty, I gently *coax* it from the counter and *wheedle* it into my pocket. Then, I sink deep into my overcoat—(*he moves to the arch*) and *edge* towards the door —where I always pause—just in case I'm called back. Then, if nothing happens, I stealthily manoeuvre the door ajar, squeeze my way out—and run like hell.

DOCTOR. Indeed! And what on earth made you imagine that a bank would be a suitable place for you, mm?

CHARLEY (*moving down* C.). I'm hanged if I know. I used to keep it under the bed.

DOCTOR (*ominously*). Yes. (*Briskly.*) Mr Stirling—much as I dislike having to put people away—in your case, I'm afraid there's no alternative.

CHARLEY (*crossing to* L. *of the* DOCTOR). What are you talking about? There's nothing the matter with *me*.

DOCTOR. Oh yes, there is. (*He puts the tips of his index fingers vertically together.*) You're balancing on a pin-point, my friend. (*He walks two fingers of his right hand along his left index finger.*) You're walking on the very edge of thin ice. Some long forgotten anxiety or repression has taken complete control of your unutilized *libido* —and the very fact that you deny losing your mother—I mean, your umbrella . . .

CHARLEY (*interrupting*). But I *haven't* lost it. It's in the hall.

DOCTOR (*impatiently*). No, no, no!

CHARLEY (*raising his voice*). Yes, yes, yes! You silly old twirp— I can show it to you.

(*He exits through the archway.* FLORENCE *enters and comes hurriedly down the stairs.*)

FLORENCE (*as she descends*). What's happened, Doctor? I could hear him shouting. (*She moves* C. *Anxiously.*) Is it anything serious?

DOCTOR (*moving below the table* R.C.). I've never met such a case. (*Emphatically.*) Even if he's as sane as I am, he should be certified at once.

FLORENCE. Oh, no!

DOCTOR. When I first came into the room, he amused himself by pulling faces at me. Then he said he didn't know who he was —that this wasn't his home—that somebody had poisoned him, that Angel's name was Blossom and that he used to keep the bank under his bed.

FLORENCE. Oh! (*She turns away to* L.C.)

(CHARLEY *enters up* R.C. *He carries his own nicely rolled umbrella.*)

CHARLEY (*moving to* L. *of the* DOCTOR). There you are.
DOCTOR (*taking the umbrella from* CHARLEY). Oh! Thank you. I was wondering where I put it.
CHARLEY (*turning to* FLORENCE *and not immediately realizing who she is*). Well! What do you know about that? (*He does a "take".*) Oh! Hullo, Florrie.
FLORENCE (*surprised and displeased*). Charley! What are *you* doing here?
CHARLEY. Henry phoned me. He said he was ill and needed my help. (*He indicates the* DOCTOR. *Emphatically.*) But if that old geyser's staying here—I'm going.
DOCTOR. Eh? What's that?
FLORENCE. Doctor. This isn't my husband—it's his brother.
DOCTOR (*picking up his bag and case and* CHARLEY'S *umbrella*). You mean, I've been dealing with the wrong fellow?
FLORENCE. Yes.
CHARLEY (*to the* DOCTOR). You and your *Oedipus Octopus*. I've half a mind to claim damages.
DOCTOR (*angrily*). I may have mistaken my patient, sir—but by heaven, my diagnosis was correct.

(*He puts on his hat and exits through the archway taking* CHARLEY'S *umbrella and leaving his stethoscope on the table* R.C.)

CHARLEY. Where on earth did you dig him up?
FLORENCE. He's not our usual doctor. He thought you were Henry.
CHARLEY (*crossing to the fireplace*). Yes, I realize that now—but would you mind telling me what's the matter with Henry? From the interview *I've* just had, it must be something very peculiar.
FLORENCE (*sitting on the sofa*). He's had a nervous breakdown.
CHARLEY. How has it taken him?
FLORENCE (*breaking down*). I don't really know—except that he came home last night without his jacket—and with lipstick on his face.
CHARLEY (*unbelievingly*). *Henry?*
FLORENCE (*tearfully*). Yes. It was his birthday.
CHARLEY. Phew! Gave himself a proper present, didn't he? But I wouldn't call that a breakdown—it was more in the nature of a break *out*.
FLORENCE. I don't wish to discuss the matter with *you*, Charley. I don't want you here at all. You've never been a good influence in the family—and, until now, you and Henry have never had the slightest thing in common. The very fact that he sent for you makes me feel quite sick with apprehension.
CHARLEY. Damn it, he's my own brother.
FLORENCE (*rising; angrily*). But he's my husband. (*She hurries to the stairs and goes up them. Tearfully.*) At least, he *was*.

(*She exits hurriedly up the stairs.* CHARLEY *crosses to the foot of the stairs.*)

CHARLEY (*calling up the stairs*). Don't you worry, Florrie. I'll look after him. That sort of illness is right down my street.

(*A door is heard to slam upstairs.* CHARLEY *shrugs his shoulders.* BERYL *flounces in through the archway. She carries a vase filled with* CHARLEY'S *flowers. She crosses and puts the vase on the table in the window. As she does so,* HENRY *is heard off, briskly singing* "Enjoy yourself!", *etc.* BERYL *hurriedly glances through the window.*)

BERYL (*hurriedly moving back from the window*). It is! It is! (*Jumping excitedly up and down.*) Oh, lovely, lovely, lovely!

(CHARLEY, *bewildered, peers cautiously round the potted palm opposite the foot of the stairs.* BERYL *exits excitedly through the archway.* CHARLEY *starts to follow her but hurriedly hides behind the palm as* HENRY *is heard to speak.*)

HENRY (*off; loudly and breezily*). Hullo, Beryl! Good heavens, you must have been waiting at the door for me.

BERYL (*off; excitedly*). I knew you hadn't the key, sir.

(HENRY *enters briskly through the archway.* BERYL *follows him on.* HENRY *wears a light grey suit, a colourful tie, has a flower in his buttonhole, and wears his hat well on one side. He smokes a cigar and carries a dispatch-case. He is now clean shaven.*)

HENRY (*as he enters; loudly and breezily*). Charming, charming! Very thoughtful of you.

(BERYL *hesitates in the arch.*)

(*He looks over his shoulder and moves* C.) Come in, little girl, don't be frightened.

(BERYL *moves to* R. *of* HENRY *and stands close to him.*)

My word, you look quite flushed. You haven't got a temperature, have you?

BERYL (*coyly*). I believe I might have, sir—in a roundabout sort of way.

HENRY (*chucking* BERYL *under the chin*). Ha, ha, ha! You and your roundabouts. You're a quaint little minx and no mistake.

BERYL (*coyly and excitedly*). Thank you, sir.

(HENRY *laughs heartily, removes his hat and puts it with his dispatch-case on the table below the stairs.*)

HENRY (*briskly*). Well, well! Where's the trouble and strife?
BERYL (*mystified*). Trouble and strife, sir?
HENRY (*moving down* L. *of the sofa*). Yes. Haven't you heard the expression? Pot and pan, the old man—trouble and strife, the

wife. Ha, ha, ha! We mustn't be too formal these days. (*He sits on the left arm of the sofa with his feet on the sofa seat.*)

BERYL (*moving to the sofa*). Oh, it's wonderful to see you laughing so free and easy, sir. And you do look lovely without the moustache.

HENRY (*breezily*). Yes, it certainly makes a difference. Quite a number of people have remarked on it. Tell me, do I look younger?

BERYL (*moving close to* HENRY). Oh, yes, sir. And ever so gay. A real lady's man, sir.

HENRY (*chuckling and wagging a finger at* BERYL). Now, now, Beryl. No flirting.

BERYL (*giggling*). As you wish, sir. (*She turns her back to* HENRY *and shyly and laughingly stoops with her face in her hand.*)

(HENRY *raises his hand to smack* BERYL's *behind*. CHARLEY *reacts.*
HENRY *restrains himself in time, rises and crosses to* C.)

(*She moves to* L. *of* HENRY.) Oh, sir, have you started on cigars?

HENRY. And why not, may I ask? A little of what you fancy does you good. Didn't you know that, Beryl? (*He laughs wickedly and puffs his cigar.*)

BERYL. Well, yes, sir—but only from what I've read about it.

(HENRY *puffs a little smoke towards* BERYL.)

Oh, my! Cigars do smell wicked, don't they? I mean—in a manly sort of way.

HENRY. Yes, they certainly give one an air, Beryl—no denying that. By Jove! Do you know what I've a particular fancy for at the moment?

BERYL (*shyly*). No, sir.

HENRY. A spanking good glass of sherry.

BERYL. Oh. Yes, sir. There is half a bottle—but it's only cooking sherry, sir.

HENRY. Let's have it.

BERYL (*surprised*). What—me as well, sir?

HENRY. Why not?

BERYL (*giggling*). I'm not used to strong drink, sir. It might get the worst of me.

HENRY Well, what if it does, eh? (*He gives her a sideways "boomps-a-daisy".*)

BERYL (*with a little scream*). Oh, Mr Stirling. (*She hurriedly moves to the arch then turns. Excitedly.*) Shall I bring the sherry in here, sir —or shall we have it in the kitchen?

HENRY. In the kitchen, by all means. Let's be Bohemian! (*He moves to* L. *of* BERYL.) But—we'd better not let Mrs Stirling know. My word, we'd be the talk of the town.

BERYL. I'll never breathe a word, sir. Oh, this is wonderful!

(*She flounces away through the archway.*)

HENRY. Ha, ha, ha! Excitable girl! (*He dances down* C. *and sings happily.*) "The world belongs to everyone but Beryl belongs to me." (*He suddenly decides to follow* BERYL, *stubs out his cigar in the ashtray on the table* R.C., *then tiptoes to the arch.*)

CHARLEY (*moving to* R. *of the sofa*). Hi, hi, hi!

(HENRY, *startled, stops and turns.*)

What are you up to?

HENRY. Upon my soul! It's Charley. You old devil! (*He moves to* R. *of* CHARLEY *and holds out his hand.*) What on earth are *you* doing here?

CHARLEY (*shaking hands*). Damn it, you asked me to come.

HENRY. Not to *my* knowledge.

CHARLEY. Didn't you phone me this morning and tell me you were worried?

HENRY. Worried? Worried? (*Loudly.*) Worried! (*Suddenly.*) Oh! (*He puts his hand to his forehead. Loudly and emotionally.*) Oh, thank heaven you've answered my call.

CHARLEY. Blimey! You do blow hot and cold, don't you?

HENRY. Ssh! (*He glances towards the arch.*) Did you hear me talking to the maid just then?

CHARLEY. I certainly did.

HENRY (*very worried*). I didn't say anything wicked, did I?

CHARLEY. No, you didn't *say* anything—but you sounded full of promise.

HENRY. Charley—I'm very ill.

CHARLEY. Personally, I'd say you were highly convalescent.

(BERYL *flounces through the archway, tremendously excited.*)

BERYL (*moving to* R. *of* HENRY). I've poured it out, sir—and drawn up two chairs. Oh, it does look cosy. (*She sees* CHARLEY.) Oh!

HENRY (*abruptly*). That will do, thank you, Beryl—you can get back to the kitchen.

BERYL. Very good, sir.

(*She half glances at* CHARLEY, *lowers her eyes, then turns and exits hurriedly through the archway.*)

CHARLEY (*incredulously*). How long has *that* little affair been going on?

HENRY. Only since this morning. But it's not what it appears, Charley. There's been nothing between us, I swear it. It's just that—something keeps coming over me in waves. One moment I'm perfectly normal—and then suddenly it's as though I'm not myself. I say things that are quite foreign to me. And I *think* things. Oh, Charley, you don't know the things I think. And sometimes I hear a voice—a voice that tells me to *do* things. That's how it started this morning with Beryl.

CHARLEY. How *what* started?
HENRY. A certain incident.
CHARLEY (*moving to the sofa*). Damn it, *tell* me—don't tease me. (*He sits on the sofa.*)
HENRY. It was about seven-thirty a.m. She had handed me the usual cup of tea—and I accidentally dropped the morning paper. In the kindness of her heart she bent to pick it up—and, in one short second, my whole nature completely changed. I became somebody quite different. I remember almost shouting, "No, don't!", but another side of me whispered, "Yes, do!", and before I realized what I was doing—I did.
CHARLEY. Did what?
HENRY. I pinched her.
CHARLEY. Where?
HENRY. In the bedroom. (*He sits on the chair* L. *of the table* R.C.)
CHARLEY. You know, you've got one of the nicest nervous breakdowns I've ever encountered.
HENRY. Charley! I came home with lipstick on my lips.
CHARLEY. I know. Florrie told me.
HENRY. I had no jacket, no bowler hat...
CHARLEY. And you'd lost that damned umbrella. Now we don't want to go into that again. When did all this nonsense first start?
HENRY. Yesterday. It was my fiftieth birthday.
CHARLEY. I know. That's why I brought you the flowers.
HENRY (*looking at the flowers on the table* R.). *You*—brought me those?
CHARLEY. That's right.
HENRY. For my birthday?
CHARLEY. Of course.

(HENRY *looks from the flowers to* CHARLEY *and starts to blink and sniff. He wipes a tear from his eye with one finger.*)

(*He rises and crosses to* L. *of* HENRY.) There, there, there! Turn it up, Henry. You'll start me off in a moment. (*He takes out his handkerchief.*) Here. Have a good blow.
HENRY (*tearfully*). Yes—that'll make me feel better. (*He takes the handkerchief from* CHARLEY *and noisily blows his nose.*)
CHARLEY. D'you remember when I used to cry as a kid? Mother *always* used to give me a handkerchief and say, "Have a good blow, it'll make you feel better".
HENRY. Yes.
CHARLEY. And just as I was in the middle of the blow, you used to pull the handkerchief away.
HENRY. I was jealous. (*He gives the handkerchief to* CHARLEY.) You were her favourite.
CHARLEY (*moving* C.). Don't talk bosh!

HENRY. You were. Always, when she said good night, you got two kisses. I only got one.

CHARLEY. Well, I was two years younger. I never *knew* you were jealous.

HENRY. I hid it.

CHARLEY. Still, it didn't stop us being good pals together, did it?

HENRY. No.

CHARLEY. Remember how we used to sing together in the choir?

HENRY (*smiling*). Yes.

CHARLEY. You always sang next to the boy who fainted.

(HENRY *reacts*.)

(*He moves to the sofa and sits on it.*) And then—we drifted apart. We didn't seem to like the same things as we grew older. You took the straight and narrow path—and I became a bit of a *bad* lad. Funny, that. Mother always thought it would be the other way round. You gave her a lot of trouble when you were a boy, you know.

HENRY. I didn't.

CHARLEY. Oh, yes you did. And *I* was a sweet curly-haired little cherub. It just goes to show, doesn't it?

HENRY. Yes.

CHARLEY. Henry, why did you send for me?

HENRY (*rising and crossing to the sofa*). Charley, you're a man of the world—I'm not. (*He sits* R. *of* CHARLEY *on the sofa*.) You know all about women and things—I don't. I need looking after, I need watching.

CHARLEY. Don't be silly! Just because you've kissed a woman who isn't your wife? Look what I have to put up with—and I'm not married. But I'm engaged.

HENRY. Who to?

CHARLEY. A little piece called Honey. She's as soft and purry as a kitten. But, oh boy, does she know how to deal with me. If she sees me out with another girl she buys herself a dress—and sends me in the bill. If she sees me holding another girl's hand she buys herself two dresses—sends me in the bill. If she sees me kissing a girl she buys herself three dresses—sends me in the bill. On one occasion which I shall never forget she bought eight dresses. That girl's got the biggest wardrobe in London. (*Laughingly*.) Ha! Don't you worry, old sport, I'll look after you.

HENRY. No. Nobody can look after me. (*He rises.*)

CHARLEY. Why not?

HENRY (*crossing to the fireplace*). Because I'm not always here to look af er.

CHARLEY. What d'you mean?

HENRY. I keep going away from myself.

CHARLEY. You know, it's a good thing you and that old doctor didn't get together. I don't know *where* you would have ended up. What time did you go out last night?

HENRY (*standing with his back to the fireplace*). At exactly eight-twenty. I left here to attend a Rotary meeting. I was walking to the bus stop when, suddenly, a wave of the most awful depression came over me. (*He crosses to* c.) I felt unutterably weary of anything to do with the routine of all the past years. In one sudden flash I realized that I had never *embraced* my life—I had only held it by the hand. Suddenly a taxi stopped right in front of me. A girl got out—and I got in.

CHARLEY. Are you absolutely certain that the girl got out before you got in?

HENRY. Oh, most definitely. She paid her fare—the flag was clicked up and down—and there I was sitting where she had been. I remember the seat was quite warm. Then I told the driver to drive like the devil—anywhere, I didn't care, and after about five minutes the taxi pulled up in a traffic jam—and there on my left, twinkling and beckoning to me, were the lights of a music-hall. It was just what I was looking for—exactly what I wanted. I sprang from the taxi, paid the fare . . .

CHARLEY (*interrupting*). How much?

HENRY. Exactly one shilling. I gave the driver one and three-pence. I remember he mumbled his thanks.

CHARLEY. That's what *you* think. What time did the show start?

HENRY. At eight-thirty. But, Charley, I was home by nine-twenty-five. What can have happened?

CHARLEY (*rising and crossing to* L. *of* HENRY). Listen, Henry. (*He leads him down* c.) From a vast experience, I can assure you that on the morning after it's quite impossible to check up every detail of the night before. You're not in the same mood. A face that looked beautiful to you at midnight can frighten the hell out of you at eight a.m. There's nothing serious the matter with you. You're suffering from a sort of immoral hangover. That's why you keep going away from yourself. You're trying to find better company. The whole thing is psychological. It's a throw back to something that happened in your youth. Tell me—can you remember any long-forgotten anxiety or repression? Anything locked up in your old *libido* that—years and years ago—caused you a deep feeling of shame?

HENRY. No. I don't think so.

CHARLEY (*aping the* DOCTOR *and putting the tips of his index fingers vertically together*). No pin points?

HENRY. No.

CHARLEY (*walking two fingers of his right hand along his left index finger*). No thin ice?

HENRY. No.

CHARLEY. Ever meet a fellow called *Oedipus?*

HENRY (*moving below the table* R.C.). Certainly not!
CHARLEY. Nothing at all?
HENRY. No. Except perhaps . . .
CHARLEY. Perhaps—*what?*
HENRY (*moving to* R. *of* CHARLEY). Only that, when I was about eleven years old, I wrote something on the bathroom wall at school. There was a terrible to-do about it. The wrong boy got blamed—and I never owned up that I was the culprit.
CHARLEY. What did you write on the wall?
HENRY (*after some hesitation*). "Silly old master."
CHARLEY (*after a moment's thought*). How did you spell "master"?
HENRY. Well, I was very young at the time . . .

(*The weird sound of the saw-violin is heard softly for a few moments.* HENRY *suddenly loosens his collar, takes out his handkerchief, mops his brow and moves above the table* R.C.)

CHARLEY (*concerned*). What's wrong?
HENRY (*whipping round; his eyes narrowing*). I hated that school! As I hate all authority. I'll let the bank know that! Rules and regulations—rotas and routine. (*He shouts and bangs the table* R.C.) To hell with them!
CHARLEY (*scared*). For the love of Pete! What's the matter with you?
HENRY (*moving to* R. *of* CHARLEY; *loudly*). I'm sick of the little world I live in! The petty safety of it nauseates me. I'd change ten years of this existence for just one week of low high-life in Paris. Nothing more satisfying than the emptiness of gaudy tinsel. (*Passionately.*) I love it! *The Bal Tabarin*, eh? What about it, Charley? Could you come away with me for a night or two?
CHARLEY. Have you gone cuckoo?
HENRY (*crossing below* CHARLEY *to* L.C.; *loudly*). Oh, there's still something of youth in me. And I've a warm attachment for the weaker sex. (*He moves to* L. *of* CHARLEY.) By Jove! Do you know what I've a particular fancy for at the moment?
CHARLEY. Don't tell me. Write it down.
HENRY (*loudly*). I'd like a spanking good glass of sherry. (*He crosses above* CHARLEY *and stands above the table* R.C.)
CHARLEY. I know. Then we all have fun and games in the kitchen.

(HENRY *suddenly sweeps everything except the glass from the table* R.C. *to the floor.*)

Henry, for heaven's sake pull yourself together!
HENRY (*loudly and indignantly*). For nearly twenty years I've lived in this one little house—and for *over* twenty years I've been faithful to my one little wife. Never a voyage on the great high seas—never a fiver carelessly thrown on the tables—and never the

sweet romance of stolen whispers under scented trees, while music softly steals from the great pagoda. But, by heaven—(*he bangs the table* R.C.) it's not too late! (*He moves to* R. *of* CHARLEY. *With a change of tone.*) Have you ever noticed how furniture can begin to look at you? Year after year, staying exactly where it's put—smug, silent and superior. It completely dominates one. (*He crosses below* CHARLEY *to* L.C. *and points to the mantelpiece.*) Look at that damn clock! It's actually smiling. It dictates my very life, my every movement. It strikes nine—and I leave for the bank. It strikes five—and I come home from the bank. It strikes ten—and I go to bed. (*He moves to the fireplace.*) Tick-tock! Tick-tock! (*At the top of his voice, to the clock.*) How *dare* you tick-tick at me? (*Suddenly and impulsively he grabs the clock from the mantelpiece and wallops it into the fireplace, then stands and stares at the wreckage.*)

(CHARLEY *staggers to the table* R.C. *and picks up the glass. He is just about to drink when he remembers his previous experience, and with a howl of dismay he replaces the glass on the table* R.C., *moves down* C. *and mops his brow with his handkerchief.*)

(*He turns and crosses to* L. *of* CHARLEY.) I've had another mood.
CHARLEY. Are you telling me!

(FLORENCE *enters and comes down the stairs.*)

FLORENCE (*as she descends*). What was that crash? (*She sees the broken clock.*) Oh! (*Tearfully.*) He always hated that clock. (*She moves down* L.) I believe you did it on purpose. (*She does not nag, but is unable to forget the lipstick.*) Why were you so late home? I've been worried sick about you. They actually phoned me from the bank. If you don't pull yourself together you'll be transferred.
HENRY (*moving* L.C.). You're wrong, Florence. If I don't pull myself together, I'll be arrested.
FLORENCE. Henry!
CHARLEY. What do you mean?
HENRY. I meant to tell you before, but I couldn't bring myself to do it. This morning—I did something terrible.
FLORENCE (*apprehensively*). What?
HENRY. I took three hundred pounds from the manager's safe.
FLORENCE. Oh, no!
CHARLEY (*moving* R. *of* HENRY). Three hundred pounds! (*Loudly.*) What did you do with it?
HENRY. I put it back.
FLORENCE (*sitting on the sofa*). Oh, thank God!

(CHARLEY *holds his forehead and staggers away to sit on the table* R.C.)

HENRY. I always have my elevenses in a room near the manager's office. I'm not supposed to—but it's just a snack and a cup of tea from my thermos. (*He moves* C.) There's a little safe in the corner which is always closed as a rule—but this morning it was open. I was just about to take the sandwiches from my despatch-case when I found myself staring at three hundred pounds in fivers. They had a rubber band with a slip of white paper round them. Suddenly, I heard myself whispering—"Three hundred pounds at ten to one would mean three thousand". And before I realized what was happening my hand moved forward, took up the notes and put them into my despatch-case. Immediately a wave of horror swept over me—and I put them back in the safe. It was then that there seemed to be two of me. One kept whispering—"Borrow them"—and the other kept whispering—"Don't". I actually *watched* my hand—going to and fro—taking the notes, putting them back—into the safe, out of the safe—into my despatch-case and out again. It went on for nearly half a minute. Finally, with a superhuman effort, I literally wrenched the notes from my case, flung them into the safe, slammed the door—and staggered away. (*He sits on the chair* L. *of the table* R.C.) Florence—that hasn't made me a thief, has it?

FLORENCE (*hiding her distress*). No, Henry. It shows that *nothing* could make you a thief. (*She rises.*) I'll make you a cup of tea.

CHARLEY (*putting his left arm around* HENRY's *shoulders*). Florrie, I think we'd better get that old doctor. I know he's nuts—but I believe he's right for *this* case.

HENRY (*rising*). No. I don't want a doctor. (*He moves to the stairs.*) I'll just go upstairs and lie down for a bit.

(BERYL *enters excitedly through the archway.*)

BERYL. If you please, ma'am, there's a gentleman to see Mr Stirling.

FLORENCE. Who is it, Beryl?

BERYL. Well, I asked him what his name was—and he said he didn't know.

(CHARLEY's *eyes cross; he rises, moves* R. *and does the 'crazy' business of trying to catch his finger.*)

FLORENCE. Show him in.
BERYL. Very good, ma'am.

(*She exits through the archway very excited.* CHARLEY *beckons to* HENRY *who crosses to* L. *of the table* R.C.)

CHARLEY. Henry, have you told us everything?
HENRY. Yes.
CHARLEY. You haven't kept a little titbit back as a surprise?
HENRY. No.
CHARLEY. Because, if you have, we're going to get it now.

(BERYL *enters and stands in the archway.*)

BERYL (*announcing*). The nameless gentleman.

(HENRY *moves to* R. *of* FLORENCE *and turns.* BOYLE *enters through the archway. He carries a lumpy brown paper parcel.*)

BOYLE (*moving* C.). Good evening, sir.

(BERYL *exits through the archway.*)

HENRY. Good evening. I seem to know your face.
BOYLE. And I seem to know yours, sir. (*He looks at* CHARLEY.)
CHARLEY. No. You don't know mine.
FLORENCE. Who *are* you?
BOYLE. Well, it's rather hard to explain, madam. I know who I am—but I can't remember my name. It's very worrying. (*He laughs; the same lugubrious haunted ghost laugh.*) That's another thing. Just because I laugh it doesn't mean that I think anything's funny. Quite the reverse—I'm very depressed. (*He laughs.*) You see, if I don't manage to *stop* this laughing, I'll lose my job.
CHARLEY (*moving below the table* R.C.). What is your job?
BOYLE. I'm an undertaker. (*He laughs.*)
CHARLEY (*ruffling his own hair*). Of course, the whole thing's a dream. I'm not here at all. I'm down town somewhere—absolutely cockeye. Taxi!
HENRY (*to* BOYLE). Why have you called here?
BOYLE. Well, sir, if you're Mr Henry Stirling—(*he holds out the parcel to* HENRY) I've got your jacket and bowler hat.

(HENRY *takes the parcel.*)

CHARLEY. Where did you find them?
BOYLE. Somebody gave them to me last night.
FLORENCE (*taking the parcel from* HENRY). Where *were* you last night?
BOYLE. That's something else I can't remember—(*to* HENRY) but I know we were together, sir.
HENRY (*amazed*). Together?
BOYLE. Oh, yes, sir.
CHARLEY. Damn it, you must remember more than that. Were you in an hotel, or a club, or what?
BOYLE. For the life of me I can't place it, sir. But I know there was a lot of fun going on. I remember somebody putting the lights out—(*he turns to* HENRY) and I remember wearing your bowler hat while you were kissing that woman.

(HENRY *closes his eyes.*)

FLORENCE. Oh! (*She throws the parcel on to the sofa and moves to the fireplace.*)
BOYLE (*to* HENRY). You enjoyed yourself, you did. I was *very* unhappy. (*He laughs.*) Then there was a free for all—and somebody broke your umbrella.
CHARLEY. Don't believe it, Florrie. He's lying.
BOYLE. It's the truth, sir. I'm just as worried as you are. (*He laughs.*)

CHARLEY (*grabbing* BOYLE *by the lapels; with a snarl*). Listen, poison-face—one more giggle from you and I'll kick you in the dentures.

(BOYLE *laughs*.)

(*He shakes* BOYLE *and shouts*.) Shut up! How did you know where to find Mr Stirling?

BOYLE. His card was in his wallet, in his jacket, sir. I only found it this morning.

FLORENCE (*moving to the door up* L.; *curtly*). Would you mind stepping in here, please? I think I might be able to help your memory.

BOYLE (*crossing above the sofa to the door up* L.). Oh, it isn't that I forget things. It's just that I can't remember.

(*He laughs and exits up* L. FLORENCE *follows him off, closing the door behind her.* HENRY *moves to the table below the stairs and picks up his despatch-case.*)

HENRY (*moving down* C. *with the case*). Charley, I made a fresh will this morning. Would you look after it, please? (*He opens the case and fumbles in it.*)

CHARLEY (*quickly*). Now don't get morbid! It must be some consolation to know that you couldn't get into a bigger mess than you're in now.

HENRY (*taking a packet from his case*). Hullo. What's this? (*Frantically.*) Three hundred pounds!

CHARLEY (*loudly*). What does that mean?

HENRY (*frantically*). It means I put my sandwiches in the safe!

He drops the case and package and collapses into CHARLEY's *arms.* BOYLE *is heard to laugh off as—*

the CURTAIN *quickly falls.*

ACT II

Scene 1

SCENE.—*The same. About 10 a.m. the following morning.*
The room has been tidied. The remains of breakfast for three are on the table R.C. *The stethoscope is on the table up* C.

When the CURTAIN *rises, it is a bright sunny day.* BERYL *is standing above the table* R.C., *stacking the dirty cups on to a tray. She wears an artificial flower in her hair. The gramophone is playing off. The tune is* "Frankie and Johnnie".

BERYL (*singing*). "He was my man—and he done me wrong." (*She giggles and claps her hands.*)

(FLORENCE *enters and comes down the stairs. She carries her handbag and a long well-filled envelope.*)

FLORENCE (*as she descends*). Beryl! Turn that gramophone off at once.
BERYL (*pleadingly*). Oh, Mrs Stirling!
FLORENCE. Did you hear what I said?

(BERYL *moves sulkily to the archway.*)

And take that stupid flower from your hair.

(BERYL *removes the flowers, sinks it into her bosom, smiles shyly at* FLORENCE *then exits through the archway.*)

(*Angrily.*) Tch!
(*The telephone rings.*)

(*She hurries to the telephone and lifts the receiver. Into the telephone.*) Hullo? . . . Who? . . .
(*The music off stops.*)

Oh, good morning, Doctor . . . Did you leave your what? . . . Your stethoscope? . . . Yes, it's here on the table . . . Yes, please do . . . No, he's still very strange . . . Well, he suddenly fell asleep at seven o'clock last night and he hasn't wakened up yet. . . . Oh, yes, he's still breathing . . . It'll relieve the what . . . But he hasn't got shingles . . . That's all right, Doctor—I'm very muddled, too. (*She replaces the receiver, crosses to the table in the window and puts the envelope in the table drawer.*)

(BERYL *enters through the archway, moves above the table* R.C. *and resumes the clearing of it.*)

You should have had that table cleared a long while ago. It's nearly ten o'clock.

BERYL. I've been waiting for the master to come down. He's usually at the bank by now.

FLORENCE (*moving* R. *of the table* R.C.). Mr Stirling isn't going to the bank this morning.

BERYL (*excitedly*). You mean—he's staying at home?

FLORENCE. Yes. So am I.

BERYL (*disappointedly*). Quite a family gathering, isn't it, madam? (*She picks up the tray and moves to the archway.*)

FLORENCE. Why are you leaving that cup and saucer?

BERYL (*turning*). I thought I'd take Mr Stirling a cup of tea. I usually do.

FLORENCE (*picking up the cup and saucer*). Well, in future, you usually don't. (*She puts the cup and saucer on the tray.*) I'm not having a repetition of yesterday's disgraceful behaviour.

BERYL. It wasn't disgraceful! It might have seemed so to *you*, but looking at it from the lonely dullness of *my* existence, it was a human contact that I shall always remember as something rather beautiful.

(FLORENCE *gasps.* BERYL, *on the verge of tears, exits through the archway.*)

HENRY (*off; calling*). Florence!

(*He enters and comes down the stairs. He wears pyjamas, a dressing-gown and slippers.*)

(*As he descends.*) Florence! (*He moves* C.) I've had the most terrible nightmare. I dreamt that the whole of my life had gone higgledy-piggledy; that I'd taken money from the bank, that I'd fooled about with a strange woman, insulted the maid, smashed the clock, and even sent for Charley.

(CHARLEY *enters and comes down the stairs. He wears a lounge suit.*)

Fancy that, eh? Charley of all people. With the life *he* leads. Imagine him looking after *me!*

(CHARLEY *moves towards the sofa.*)

CHARLEY (*passing* R. *of* HENRY). Good morning.

HENRY. Good morning. (*He does a "take".*) Oh, no! (*To* FLORENCE. *In a whisper.*) It isn't true, is it?

FLORENCE. Yes, Henry. It's true.

HENRY (*collapsing on to the chair* L. *of the table* R.C.). Ohhhhhh!

CHARLEY (*sitting on the sofa; breezily*). Good morning, Florrie.

FLORENCE (*curtly*). Good morning. (*She sits on the chair above the table* R.C.)

HENRY. Did I dream it, or did a man call last night who couldn't remember his name?
FLORENCE. Yes. I questioned him for half an hour.
HENRY. Did he tell you anything?
FLORENCE. Nothing that I wanted to know. *He* seemed quite mental, too. How could you choose such company?
CHARLEY. Leave him alone, Florrie. He hasn't had any breakfast yet.
HENRY (*turning to* CHARLEY). What's the time?
CHARLEY (*glancing at his wrist-watch*). Ten o'clock.
HENRY. Oh! I should be at the bank! (*He rises and hurries to the archway.*)
CHARLEY. Wo, wo, wo! You can't go like that.
FLORENCE. You can't go at all.

(HENRY *turns back.*)

HENRY (*panic-stricken*). But, my sandwiches. I must let Mr Jackson know.
FLORENCE. He knows already—I phoned him first thing this morning.
HENRY (*moving* C.). What?
CHARLEY (*to* FLORENCE). That was a damn silly thing to do.
HENRY. What did he say?
FLORENCE. I explained that you were ill, and he advised you to take things easy.
CHARLEY. And what did he say about Henry taking things easily yesterday?
FLORENCE. He said he would go into that when he called here.
HENRY. What?
FLORENCE. He's coming round to see you. You'd better get dressed.

(HENRY *moves miserably to the stairs and goes up two steps.*)

CHARLEY (*to* FLORENCE). Why didn't you let me shove those notes into the *night* safe? At least they would have been safely back in the bank.
FLORENCE. And how would Henry have explained the sandwiches?

(HENRY *stops on the second stair and looks back.*)

CHARLEY (*irritably*). They hadn't got his name and address on them, had they? And suppose they don't *find* any sandwiches?
FLORENCE. What are you hinting at?
CHARLEY. Mice. *One big mouse*—with a reasonable appetite—and Henry gets fifteen years.
FLORENCE. Now you're talking nonsense.

HENRY (*hurrying down the stairs, to* C.). No, no! He's not! The night watchman caught three this week. And, only last Thursday, one got into the big vault safe and ate two thousand pounds' worth of post-war credits.

CHARLEY. Well, nobody's going to lose anything through that. I think he *ought* to go to the bank. (*He rises.*) Come on, Henry, get dressed, and I'll go with you.

FLORENCE (*rising*). Oh, no, you won't. (*She moves to the table in the window and takes the envelope from the drawer.*) I would rather you stayed here and explained to Henry—and myself—how you managed to reduce that three hundred pounds to exactly two hundred and ninety. (*She moves below the table* R.C.)

CHARLEY. Who, me?

FLORENCE. Yes, you.

CHARLEY. How dare you!

FLORENCE. You saw me put the money into this envelope last night, and you saw me put the envelope into that drawer. When I counted it again this morning, there were two five-pound notes missing.

HENRY. Charley! *You* didn't take them, did you?

CHARLEY. Certainly not!

FLORENCE. Of course, he did. (*To* CHARLEY.) What did you do with them?

CHARLEY (*ashamed*). I went to the dogs, at Hendon.

HENRY (*closing his eyes*). Oh, no!

FLORENCE (*moving to the table in the window*). And, of course, lost every penny. (*She replaces the envelope in the drawer and closes it.*)

CHARLEY (*cheerfully*). You're wrong, Florrie. I backed a little bitch called *Lipstick*.

(HENRY *reacts.*)

She came in at five to one. I made fifty quid. (*He takes two five-pound notes from his wallet.*) Here are your two fivers. (*He crosses below* HENRY *to* L. *of* FLORENCE.) I was going to put them back myself as soon as I got the chance. (*He hands the notes to* FLORENCE.)

FLORENCE (*curtly*). Thank you.

CHARLEY. Aren't you going to put them in the envelope?

FLORENCE. Why? (*She puts the notes in her handbag.*)

CHARLEY. Well, aren't you going to make up the three hundred?

FLORENCE (*abruptly*). I've already *made* it up—from my *own* money.

HENRY (*suddenly looking foxy*). Charley. (*He moves to* L. *of* CHARLEY *and pulls him by the arm.*)

CHARLEY (*turning to* HENRY). Yes.

HENRY. Did you say you put ten pounds on at five to one?

CHARLEY. That's right.

HENRY. And you made fifty pounds clear?
CHARLEY. Yes.
HENRY. By Jove! If we had put the three hundred on we'd have made a spanking fifteen hundred pounds.
FLORENCE. Oh!
HENRY (*excitedly*). Sixty ponies. Think of it! Then if we could have found another fast little bitch like *Lipstick*, we could have made a fortune.
CHARLEY. Shut up!
FLORENCE (*really letting go*). This isn't illness. (*To* CHARLEY.) It's nothing but *your* influence.
CHARLEY. Cor blimey! (*He crosses below* HENRY *to* L.) Now you've put *me* in the wrong.
FLORENCE (*to* HENRY). If he doesn't leave this house at once, I do.

(HENRY *looks helplessly at* CHARLEY.)

CHARLEY (*sitting on the sofa*). I'm sorry, Henry, but—for a very good reason—I'm staying.
FLORENCE (*to* HENRY). What do you say to that?
HENRY (*moving* C.). What *can* I say? You're my wife—he's my brother. It isn't even Hobson's choice. I'm torn between *Scylla* and *Charybdis*.
FLORENCE. Are you sure you don't mean—Angel and Florence? (*She makes for the stairs.*)
HENRY (*moving up* C.). Oh, what a wicked thing to say!
FLORENCE (*stopping on the stairs*). I think it will even things up a bit if I persuade mother to stay here, too.

(*She hurries up the stairs and exits.*)

HENRY (*frantically*). No! Not that! Oh, Florence, I beg you! (*He turns.*) Charley, for heaven's sake, you've got to go at once.
CHARLEY. I can't.
HENRY (*moving to* R. *of the sofa*). But, you must! You've no idea what her mother's like. She *thrives* on hating *me*.
CHARLEY. Never mind about that. Listen! I've found out where you went on Thursday.
HENRY. What? (*He sits* R. *of* CHARLEY *on the sofa.*) Where?
CHARLEY (*slowly*). Have you ever heard of a hypnotist called—Mendoza?

(*There is a moment's pause, then* HENRY *screams.*)

(*He smothers* HENRY's *scream by putting his hand over* HENRY's *mouth.*) Ssh! He properly put it across you last Thursday. You went to the *Kilbane Empire*. That's how you got the lipstick from Angel, and that's why you nearly fiddled the safe. You're suffering from delayed psychic suggestion. You're a sort of male Trilby, only for God's sake don't start trying to sing.

HENRY. How did you find out all this?

CHARLEY. Well, last night, I came back early from the dogs—I never stay late if I have a win—and I suddenly thought I'd go through the pockets of your jacket, and I found (*producing it*)—this programme.

HENRY (*taking the programme and reading it*). "*The Kilbane Empire.*"

CHARLEY (*rising*). The rest was easy. I hopped down to the *Empire*, saw the show, went round the back, and had a ten-minute chat with Angel. (*He takes a small thin book from his pocket.*) I pinched this from her dressing-room.

HENRY (*taking the book and reading the title*). "*Oriental Manifestations and Principles of Magnetic Hypnotism.*"

CHARLEY (*taking the book from* HENRY). Exciting, isn't it? And it might come in very handy.

HENRY. Oh? How?

CHARLEY (*crossing to* C.). Well, Angel promised to send Mendoza round to depixilate you this afternoon, but, if he *doesn't* turn up, I'm going to have a go myself. (*He opens the book.*) Here it is. Page forty-eight. (*He reads.*) "Alternative method of depossession in cases of hysterical auto-suggestion. Sit the patient in an insulated chair and apply the electric current to his solar plexus. Ignore any screams. As soon as sparks appear in the region of his articulam . . ."

HENRY (*rising*). No! You're not doing that to me.

CHARLEY (*turning the page*). There are dozens of alternatives. What about this one? (*He reads.*) "Plunge a poker into the fire and leave until it is red hot." (*He pauses.*)

(HENRY *looks suspicious.*)

HENRY. And what happens then?

CHARLEY. Just a moment. (*He studies the instructions and his eyes open wide. He laughs.*)

HENRY. Well?

CHARLEY. I'll have to get somebody to help me.

HENRY (*putting out his hand for the book*). Why, what does it say?

CHARLEY (*moving away below the table* R.C.). No! You're not supposed to know anything about it. (*He reads.*) "For the success of this operation, it is essential that the patient be taken by surprise."

HENRY. Thank you, I've had quite enough surprises already. (*He turns and makes for the stairs.*)

CHARLEY. What are you going to do?

HENRY. Explain the whole thing to Florence.

CHARLEY (*moving to* R. *of* HENRY). Don't you know that wives never believe true explanations? She'll go straight down to check it with Angel. Do you know what will happen then?

HENRY. No.

CHARLEY. Blackmail! Mendoza will cook up a nice fruity scandal and make you pay through the nose.

HENRY. Can't I even explain to the bank?
CHARLEY (*putting his arm around* HENRY's *shoulders and leading him down* C.). Have you forgotten what you were saying just now about putting three hundred pounds on a dog? You're not fit to make explanations.
HENRY. You mean, I'm still uncertain?
CHARLEY. Your uncertainty is the only reliable thing about you. You're still *full* of possibilities. Imagine yourself in the manager's office. "I'm perfectly well now, Mr Jackson." Then his secretary drops her pencil, stoops down to pick it up, and you have one of your moods. (*He acts a slap at the secretary.*)
HENRY. Oh, surely not! That couldn't happen again, could it?
CHARLEY (*solemnly*). At any moment, without the slightest warning, your psychological bell may ring.

(*The telephone bell rings. The coincidence terrifies* HENRY *who moves quickly down* L. *in front of the sofa.* CHARLEY *moves to the telephone and lifts the receiver.*)

(*Into the telephone.*) Hullo? ... Who? ... Honey? ... Oh, darling, this is lovely. I was just going to ring *you* ... What, my sweet? ... No, darling, I'm with my brother, Henry. I left you a note on the dressing-table—phone number, address and everything ... Well, I didn't want you to wake up and not know where I was ... But, Honey-Pot, I swear it's Henry! You can talk to him if you like ... But, darling! Listen! Hullo? Hullo? Hullo? (*He angrily replaces the receiver and moves down to* HENRY.) Women! They don't believe a word you tell them. D'you know, Henry, I can't be away for a single night without Honey wanting to know what I've been doing.
HENRY (*coldly*). I thought you said she was your fiancée?
CHARLEY. That's right. What's wrong?
HENRY (*unhappily*). Nothing.

(BERYL *flusters excitedly into the archway.*)

BERYL. Please, sir, a gentleman's called. He knows his name—but he doesn't want to give it.
HENRY (*moving close to* L. *of* CHARLEY). It's Mr Jackson.

(DETECTIVE INSPECTOR MARTIN *strides in through the archway to* C. *He is a severe type, with no sense of humour. He carries his hat. He jerks his head to* BERYL *who exits hurriedly through the archway.*)

CHARLEY (*to* HENRY; *out of the corner of his mouth*). Is it?
HENRY (*out of the corner of his mouth*). No.
MARTIN. I hope I'm not interrupting?
CHARLEY. No, no. We were expecting you.
MARTIN (*very surprised*). Were you?
CHARLEY. I think so. (*To* HENRY. *Out of the corner of his mouth.*) Were we?

HENRY (*out of the corner of his mouth*). No. Not now.
MARTIN (*to* CHARLEY). You don't even know who I am, do you?
CHARLEY (*to* HENRY; *out of the corner of his mouth*). Do we?
HENRY (*out of the corner of his mouth*). Not yet.
MARTIN. I didn't give the maid my name—because I don't like frightening people. (*He puts his hat on the table* R.C. *and moves below it.*) I've called to see a Mr Henry Stirling.

(HENRY *moans.*)

(*He swings round.*) What's the matter?
CHARLEY. He's got toothache.
MARTIN (*to* HENRY). Would you rather I postponed my visit?
HENRY. No, no! Let's get it over and done with.
MARTIN (*to* HENRY). Are *you* Mr Henry Stirling?
HENRY (*to* CHARLEY; *out of the corner of his mouth*). Am I?
CHARLEY (*out of the corner of his mouth*). Well, I'm not.
HENRY (*out of the corner of his mouth*). Well, why should I tell him?
CHARLEY (*out of the corner of his mouth*). I'm not going to get into trouble for you. (*He mutters ad lib. Suddenly, to* MARTIN.) Who are *you?*
MARTIN. I'm Detective Inspector Martin.

(HENRY *gives a little scream, totters backwards and sits on the sofa.*)

What's the matter with him?
CHARLEY. Toothache.
MARTIN. Is he scared about having it out?
CHARLEY. No, he took it out yesterday. He's been wondering how he can put it back.
MARTIN. Something's frightened him very badly.
CHARLEY. No. He always looks like that.

(HENRY *rises and moves to* L. *of* CHARLEY.)

HENRY (*out of the corner of his mouth*). Don't let it get into the papers.
CHARLEY (*out of the corner of his mouth*). Shut up!
MARTIN (*moving* C.). You know, there's something funny going on here. I merely called to know if Mr Stirling could advise me about a man who's lost his memory and keeps laughing. He looked in at the station this morning to see if *we* could help him. (*To* HENRY.) All he could remember then—was your name and address.
CHARLEY. You mean—that's *all* you've called about?
MARTIN. Yes.
HENRY. Nothing else?
MARTIN. No.

(CHARLEY *and* HENRY *turn to face each other and laugh with relief ad lib.* MARTIN *moves to* R. *of* CHARLEY. HENRY *notices* MARTIN *and nudges* CHARLEY. CHARLEY *turns, then quickly moves* HENRY *between himself and* MARTIN.)

(*He turns* HENRY *round to face him.*) I happen to mention that I'm a detective—and you nearly faint. Now, why should that be?
CHARLEY. He thought you'd called about the money.
(HENRY *reacts.* CHARLEY *kicks himself.*)
MARTIN. Oh? What money?
HENRY. Just some money.
MARTIN (*quickly*). How much?
HENRY. Three hundred pounds.
MARTIN (*quickly*). Does it belong to you?
HENRY. Good heavens, no!
MARTIN (*quickly*). You didn't steal it, did you?
HENRY. No, not exactly.
MARTIN (*quickly*). What do you mean—"not exactly"?
HENRY. Well—I—er . . .
MARTIN (*angrily*). *Did you steal it?*
HENRY. Well, only in a roundabout way.
MARTIN (*ominously*). *Yes!* I'm going to look further into this. I think it's worth reporting to headquarters. (*He crosses below* HENRY *to* R. *of* CHARLEY.) Is there anything else *you'd* like to tell me?
(CHARLEY *looks innocent and tries to whistle unconcernedly, but no noise comes.*)
O.K. I'll be seeing you two gentlemen again. (*He turns, crosses briskly to the table* R.C., *picks up his hat, then moves to the arch and turns.*) I've got an idea there's something here that's going to mean promotion.
(*He slams his hat on to his head and exits through the archway.* CHARLEY *and* HENRY *sit on the sofa,* HENRY R. *of* CHARLEY.)
HENRY. Heaven help me, what have you done?
CHARLEY. I'm sorry.
HENRY. You've stirred my cup of bitterness with a sword of Damocles.
CHARLEY. I only made a little slip.
HENRY. That's all right. I don't really mind. If Florence's mother is coming here, I'd rather do six months.
CHARLEY. Now you're looking on the bright side.
(*The telephone bell rings.*)
That'll be Honey. She always checks up twice. Tell her what I'm doing here. She thinks I'm on the loose.
(HENRY *rises, moves to the telephone and lifts the receiver.* CHARLEY *rises, follows and stands* L. *of* HENRY.)
HENRY (*into the telephone*). Hullo . . . ? Yes, who's speaking . . . ? Yes, that's right. Charley thought it would be you—he said you always checked up twice . . .
(CHARLEY *reacts.*)

I don't really know about last night. I think he went to Hendon.
  CHARLEY (*in a loud whisper*). Don't mention the dogs.
  HENRY (*into the telephone*). No, no. That's wrong. He didn't go to Hendon. (*He covers the mouthpiece with his hand. To* CHARLEY.) Where *did* you go?
  CHARLEY. To the music-hall, of course.
  HENRY (*into the telephone*). Yes, that's right. He went to a music-hall . . . No, no. He wasn't with a woman. I mean, apart from the ten minutes in the dressing-room.

(CHARLEY *groans, leans sideways over the banister rail and "plays the harp" on the uprights.*)

Hullo? Hullo? Hullo? (*He replaces the receiver.*) That's funny. She rang off.

(CHARLEY *closes his eyes.*)

  CHARLEY. So help me, I believe you did that on purpose!
  HENRY. I only told her the truth.
  CHARLEY (*furiously*). I warned you less than five minutes ago. *Never* tell a woman the truth. (*He moves down* L.C.) What you've stirred up in my cup of char is *nobody's* business.

(BERYL *flounces in through the archway.*)

  BERYL (*smiling at* HENRY). There's a Mr Jackson to see you, sir.
  HENRY (*moving down* C.). Oh, no!
  CHARLEY (*moving below the sofa*). Who's Mr Jackson?
  HENRY (*moving close to* R. *of* CHARLEY; *dramatically and hopelessly*). My manager!

(STANLEY JACKSON *storms in through the archway. He is aged about forty-five. He is bald. He has every possibility of being pleasant and likeable when not in the present raging temper. He wears a trilby hat and carries a small packet of sandwiches.*)

  JACKSON (*as he enters; to* HENRY). *What* have you been doing? (*He takes off his hat and strides to* R. *of* HENRY.) You bald-headed Barabbas!

(BERYL *exits nervously through the archway.*)

(*He waves the packet of sandwiches at* HENRY.) Sandwiches! In my safe! What the hell have you been up to? Where's that money?
  HENRY (*crossing below* JACKSON *to the table in the window*). I've got it, Mr Jackson.

(JACKSON *moves below the table* R.C.)

(*He takes the envelope from the table drawer.*) It's all here. (*He moves to* R. *of* JACKSON *and holds out the envelope.*) Three hundred pounds, sir, and not a penny missing.
  JACKSON (*snatching the envelope; sarcastically*). Splendid! I can't thank you enough. And now, I suppose—(*he slaps the packet of*

sandwiches on to the table R.C.) if you check your sandwiches, everything will be all right. (*Storming*.) Do you know who was with me when I opened that safe? Mr Montague Billing.

(CHARLEY *moves* L.C.)

HENRY. No!

JACKSON. Yes! Montague Billing. (*He turns to* CHARLEY.) Director-in-Chief of all our branches. He asked me to cash him a personal cheque for three hundred pounds—and I opened the safe and gave him those sandwiches. (*He holds his forehead*.) There must be something the matter with me. I even gave him the piece of parsley. (*He flings his hat on to the floor at his feet*.)

HENRY. Mr Jackson, I can't express my remorse. (*He picks up the hat and hands it back*.)

JACKSON (*snatching the hat*). Will you leave things alone! (*He flings the hat on to the floor*.)

HENRY (*backing* R.). I'm sorry, sir. I haven't been very well for the last two days.

JACKSON (*shouting*). I haven't been well for the last five years. But I try to keep my wits about me. (*He moves to* L. *of* HENRY.) D'you think I *like* this sort of upset? Do you imagine I get a kick out of finding my chief cashier behaving like an idiot. Eh? (*He turns, sees his hat on the floor, takes a flying kick at it, then moves to the arch*.)

CHARLEY (*crossing to* L. *of* JACKSON). Let him off lightly, sir. He's a very sick man.

JACKSON (*glaring at* CHARLEY). In the banking world, we're all sick men. Managers used to have hearts inside them. Now they've only got ulcers. (*He points to* HENRY.) Look at him! In his pyjamas at half past ten. (*He moves down* C.) Stirling! If it hadn't been for your *name*, you'd have lost your job this morning. What would your wife have had to say to that? Or don't you care about her any more?

CHARLEY (*moving to* L. *of* JACKSON). I can vouch for that, sir. I'm his brother and I should know. (*He crosses below* JACKSON *to* L. *of* HENRY.) You love your wife very dearly—don't you, Henry?

HENRY (*with a break in his voice*). Of course I do. (*His tone of voice suddenly changes and he smiles wickedly*.) I love *all* women.

(JACKSON *and* CHARLEY *react, as a horrified* HENRY *realizes what he has said*.)

CHARLEY (*feebly, to* JACKSON). He's still got a brave sense of humour.

JACKSON Then, I think he should have it removed. (*To* HENRY.) You'd better take a few days leave. See a doctor—see two or three doctors—and get them to tell you the truth.

HENRY. I'll be quite normal this evening, sir. It's only a matter of a red-hot poker.

(JACKSON *reacts*.)

No, no! What am I saying?

JACKSON (*controlling himself with difficulty*). I'm going to pretend that I haven't heard *anything*. For the sake of a fifteen-year association, I'm going to pretend that I haven't called here at all. I'll just take these notes back to Mr Billing. (*He moves to the arch.*) You can explain the details to him later.

CHARLEY (*moving to* L. *of* JACKSON). I'm sure he'll understand, sir. I remember once—when I had to see a Director about an overdraft without security . . .

JACKSON (*turning; unable to believe his ears*). An overdraft without *what*?

CHARLEY. Without security. (*He smiles.*) I've been running one for years.

(JACKSON *gives a muffled scream and staggers off through the archway.*
FLORENCE *enters and comes down the stairs. She wears outdoor clothes and carries her handbag and a small suitcase.*)

FLORENCE (*as she descends; nervily*). What was that screaming?
CHARLEY (*moving down* R.C.). I didn't hear anything.
HENRY. Florence! You're not going to leave me?
FLORENCE (*moving down* L.C. *and putting the suitcase on the floor*). I'm going round to mother's, Henry. Whether I come back or not depends on whether she's willing to come back with me.
HENRY (*crossing to* C.). But you can't desert me like this!
FLORENCE. I'm not deserting you, I'm protecting you. (*She opens her handbag.*) And when Mr Jackson calls about the three hundred pounds—(*she takes out a wad of fivers and holds them up*) you can tell him to come to me for it.

(CHARLEY *and* HENRY *react.*)

You know the address. (*She replaces the wad in her handbag.*)
HENRY (*moving to* R. *of* FLORENCE; *frantically*). But, surely, the money was in that drawer there.
FLORENCE. Oh, no, it wasn't!
HENRY. What?
FLORENCE (*picking up the suitcase*). After finding ten pounds missing this morning, did you really think I would leave it there—(*she crosses below* HENRY *to* R. *of him and glares at* CHARLEY) so that Charley could help himself again? Oh, no! Ever since eight-thirty a.m. that three hundred pounds has been in my handbag. (*She turns and moves to the archway.*)
HENRY (*shouting frantically*). Then what did I give . . . ?
CHARLEY (*shouting*). What was in that long envelope?
FLORENCE (*stopping in the archway and turning; emphatically*). Fifty sheets of paper from the bathroom.

(*She exits through the archway as* HENRY *screams.* CHARLEY *clutches his forehead and collapses on to the chair* L. *of the table* R.C.)

QUICK CURTAIN

Scene 2

Scene.—*The same. Two hours later.*

When the Curtain *rises the stage is empty. The sun is still shining brightly, though from a different angle. The vase of flowers from the table in the window, and the stethoscope are on the table* R.C. Charley *enters and comes briskly down the stairs, humming a tune. As he reaches the foot of the stairs the front door is heard to slam off.* Charley *immediately stands still and listens.*

Beryl (*off*). I don't think it's any good waiting, miss.
Honey (*off*). What's the time?
Beryl (*off*). It's long past twelve, miss.
Honey (*off*). That's all right, I'll wait.
Beryl (*off*). What was the name again, miss?
Honey (*off*). Well, he knows me as Honey.

(Charley *bolts for his life up the stairs as* Honey *enters through the archway. She is aged about twenty-five, very attractive and faultlessly dressed, and possibly "sweet and purry" when her claws are not out, as they are now. As she enters she sees the flowers.*)

Where did *those* come from?
    Beryl (*coming above the table*). Mr Charley bought them for Mr Henry, miss.
    Honey. The rat! I bought them myself—for *him!* (*She moves towards the settee.*) Take them away.
    Beryl (*picking up the vase of flowers*). Very good, miss.
    Honey. Where *is* Mr Charley—do you know?
    Beryl. No, miss, except that he's not in. I think he's out.
    Honey. Didn't he say where he was going?
    Beryl. No, miss, but he looked as though he wouldn't be back for some long time.
    Honey. Why? Was he dressed for the tropics? (*She sits on the sofa.*)
    Beryl. Yes, miss. (*She moves to the arch.*)
    Honey. What's your name?
    Beryl (*stopping and turning*). Beryl, miss.
    Honey. Charming. Tell me, Beryl, what time did Mr Charley come in last night?
    Beryl (*moving* c. *level with the sofa*). Oh, I couldn't have known that, miss. I was in bed.
    Honey. That needn't necessarily mean a thing. How was he this morning?
    Beryl. Well, not exactly *comme il faut*, miss. Nothing serious, of course, just a suggestion of *malaise*, with a slight *mal de tête*.
    Honey. I can only presume that you don't *know* the French for blood-shot eyes.
    Beryl. No, miss.

(*The front-door bell is heard to ring off.*)

Excuse me, miss.

(*She exits through the archway, taking the vase of flowers with her.* HONEY *glances round. She sees the stethoscope on the table* R.C., *rises, picks it up, holds it with two fingers and wonders if it is anything to do with* CHARLEY. *The front door bangs.* HONEY *throws the stethoscope on the table, moves to the arch, stands just above it and looks off* L. CHARLEY *enters and comes happily down the stairs, thinking the door slam was her exit. He catches sight of her in the arch, reacts violently, turns and tears noisily up the stairs.* HONEY *whips round, moves quickly* C. *and looks up the stairs, but does not see anybody. A door is heard to slam upstairs.* HONEY *exits quickly up the stairs. As she does so,* BERYL *enters through the archway followed by the* DOCTOR. *He carries his hat and medical bag.*)

(*She stands up* R. *and points to the table* R.C.) There it is, Doctor, safe and sound.

DOCTOR (*moving to* L. *of the table* R.C., *putting his hat and bag on it and picking up the stethoscope*). You naughty little fellow! Why do you do it, eh? Always trying to hide from Daddy. I'll have to give you a jolly good wigging. It's no good hanging your head.

BERYL. Are you all right, sir?

DOCTOR. Er, yes, yes. You get on with your work. I'll just phone my surgery. I believe I left my stethoscope . . (*He realizes he has the stethoscope in his hand.*) Oh, dear, oh, dear! What *is* the matter with me? (*He puts the stethoscope on the table.*) I'll have to see a doctor. I wish I knew a good one.(*To* BERYL.) Get me a glass of water, will you? I think I'll take an aspirin.

BERYL. Very good, sir.

(*She exits through the archway.* HONEY *enters and comes down the stairs. She is more angry than suspicious. The* DOCTOR *turns.*)

DOCTOR (*brightly*). Ah! Mrs Stirling. How are you? (*He puts on his pince-nez.*) It *is* Mrs Stirling, isn't it?

HONEY (*moving down* L.C.). Heaven knows, it *should* be.

DOCTOR (*moving* C.). Splendid! I wasn't certain for a moment. You look so much younger. No need to ask how *Mr* Stirling is. (*He beams at* HONEY.) His health is reflected in your face.

HONEY. I must look like hell!

DOCTOR. And how is the sleeping business now? More natural, I hope?

HONEY. I wouldn't know how to answer that.

DOCTOR. Oh, dear. No improvement? Still not waiting until he gets into bed? I've been very worried about that going to sleep standing up business. It's quite outside *my* experience.

HONEY. Mine, too. I must ask him about it.

DOCTOR (*moving* HONEY *down* C.; *lowering his voice*). He hasn't been fooling about with the maid again, has he?

HONEY. I wouldn't be surprised.

(BERYL *enters through the archway and moves to* R. *of the* DOCTOR. *She carries a glass of water.*)

DOCTOR (*to* BERYL; *absent-mindedly*). Yes, yes, three times a day. (*He takes the glass from* BERYL.) I mean, thank you. (*Very annoyed with himself, he crosses below* BERYL *to the table* R.C., *puts the glass on it and fiddles in his waistcoat pocket.*)
HONEY. Beryl, are you certain Mr Charley isn't upstairs?
BERYL. I'll go and make sure, if you like.
HONEY. Yes, Beryl. Go and make sure.

(BERYL *moves to the stairs.*)

DOCTOR (*still fiddling; muttering, to* HONEY). You don't happen to know what I'm looking for, do you?
BERYL (*stopping on the second stair*). You said something about taking an aspirin.

(*She exits up the stairs.*)

DOCTOR. Ah, yes! Of course. That was why I wanted the water. (*He picks up his hat and bag.*) Well, well, I must be off. (*He moves* C.) Good-bye, dear lady—(*confidentially*) and take a little advice from an old man. Get rid of that brother. What do they call him? Charley, that's it.

(HONEY *reacts.*)

Oh, what a bad egg! (*He lowers his voice.*) Up to some nonsense with a girl called Blossom. He told me himself. Disgraceful!

(BERYL *comes flustering down the stairs and moves to* L. *of* HONEY.)

BERYL. I've just remembered where Mr Charley went to. He's playing golf.
HONEY. Where?
BERYL. On the golf course.
DOCTOR. Splendid! Nothing better.
HONEY (*icily*). Which golf course, Beryl?
BERYL. Er—it's somewhere near Finchley, I think.
DOCTOR (*to* HONEY). Ah! I'm going to a nursing-home at Finchley. Yes, I'm operating this afternoon. I can give you a lift if you like. I know the golf course well.
HONEY. Thank you.
DOCTOR. But where are your clubs?
HONEY. I'm not playing.
DOCTOR. Ah, well, never mind—you can watch me.

(*He puts on his hat and exits, with his bag, through the archway.*)

HONEY (*to* BERYL). If by any chance I don't find Mr Charley, tell him I called, will you?

BERYL. Very well, miss. Shall I give him your love?

HONEY (*livid*). No. I'll give him everything myself, when I see him.

(*She turns and exits through the archway.* BERYL *is about to hurry towards the stairs when she sees the stethoscope. She picks it up and hurries to the arch. As she does so,* CHARLEY *enters, and comes down the stairs.*)

BERYL (*calling through the arch*). Oh, Doctor...

CHARLEY (*leaning over the banisters*). Sss! Sss!

(BERYL *turns.*)

Have they gone?

BERYL. Yes, sir. Miss Honey didn't seem very upset. She was smiling.

CHARLEY (*coming down the stairs*). Oh, dear! Look out, boys! What have you got there?

BERYL (*moving* R.C.). It's the doctor's stethoscope, sir. He's forgotten it again, and he said he couldn't work without it.

CHARLEY (*taking the stethoscope from* BERYL). How the hell he can work with it beats me. (*He blows down one of the tubes and the stethoscope gives him a "bronx cheer". He looks startled and hands the stethoscope to* BERYL.)

BERYL (*putting the stethoscope on the table* R.C.). Is Mr Henry still sleeping?

CHARLEY. Like a log. I've tried everything I know—and I can't wake him.

BERYL (*moving close to* R. *of* CHARLEY). There *must* be something the matter, sir.

CHARLEY. There is. In strictest confidence, Beryl, on Thursday night, he was hypnotized. D'you know what that means?

BERYL. Oh, yes, sir. What my sister was by a soldier.

CHARLEY. No, no, no! You're thinking of compromised. (*He crosses above* BERYL *to the chair* L. *of the table* R.C. *and turns the chair to face* L. *He points to the chair and smiles.*) Sit down, Beryl.

(BERYL, *nervous and apprehensive, sits in the chair.* CHARLEY *smiles at her, pats her left shoulder and moves* C. *as he pulls the Hypnotism book from his pocket.*)

I'm just going to put you to sleep.

BERYL (*very frightened*). Oh, sir!

CHARLEY (*soothingly*). Only for five minutes. It'll give you a nice rest. (*He opens the book, studies it for a few moments then suddenly lunges his right hand towards* BERYL.)

(BERYL *starts back, terrified.*)

Look at my eyes! They are growing smaller. (*He makes mystic passes with his hand in front of* BERYL's *face.*) You're going to sleep. You're going to sleep. You're going to sleep. You're asleep.

(BERYL's *eyes close. The front-door bell is heard to ring off.*)

BERYL (*opening her eyes and rising*). Excuse me, sir.

(*She exits through the archway.* CHARLEY *looks depressed and defeated. He studies the book again, and turns a page.*)

CHARLEY (*reading and moving* L.). "If difficulty is experienced when attempting to rouse the patient from deep slumber, it is sometimes advisable to seek the help of a stronger personality." (*To himself. Musingly, as he turns the page.*) Now who can we suggest for that?

(BERYL *enters through the archway and stands* R. *of the arch.*)

BERYL (*announcing*). Mr Henry's mother-in-law, Mrs Whittle, sir.

(MRS WHITTLE *surges into the archway. She is handsome, large and dominating. She is smartly dressed. She carries an umbrella and a handbag.*)

CHARLEY (*as* MRS WHITTLE *enters*). Cor blimey, yes! (*He turns to the arch.*) That old floosie would do it. (*He sees* MRS WHITTLE *and nearly collapses.*)

(BERYL *gasps and exits hurriedly through the archway.*)

MRS WHITTLE. *What* did you call me?

(CHARLEY *tries to say something but no sound comes.*)

(*She moves down* L.C.) You thieving parasite! Not content with your dissipation at Richmond, you deliberately get in touch with Henry to lead *him* astray. How *dare* you force your way into this house? It's my daughter's home, as well as your brother's. I always knew, when Florence married Henry, we'd have you to deal with as well. I haven't yet forgotten that wedding. As the clergyman gave his blessing, you hiccupped. And then, at the breakfast, your artful nudgings and knowing winks. Oh! I was so ashamed. And now, like something from underneath a stone, you come into my life again. I don't suppose Florence has told me everything, her modesty wouldn't permit it, but she's told me enough. Stealing money, rolling home drunk, introducing your baggages to Henry. But—(*she pokes* CHARLEY *in the ribs with her umbrella*) you're——

(CHARLEY *giggles ticklishly.*)

—not satisfied with that. No! You intend to stay here. Breaking up a marriage means nothing to rakes like you. If I were a man I'd horsewhip you. Just let me meet that loose-living fallen angel. I'll clip her wings for her. If there's one thing evil in this world, 't's a woman who comes between husband and wife. Especially when she's the husband's brother's ex-mistress.

CHARLEY (*shocked*). Oh!

MRS WHITTLE. Don't argue with *me*. (*She moves* C.) Where's Henry?

CHARLEY (*pointing upstairs; feebly*). Upstairs.

MRS WHITTLE. What's he doing?

CHARLEY. Sleeping.

MRS WHITTLE. Who with? (*Immediately—and furious with herself.*) I mean—where?

CHARLEY. In his bedroom.

MRS WHITTLE (*shuddering*). Ugh! You make the very word sound disgusting. (*She moves to the staircase, goes up one stair, then stops and turns.*) Has the bank manager called yet?

CHARLEY. No.

MRS WHITTLE. Well, when he does, you can tell him *I* have his three hundred pounds.

CHARLEY (*moving up* L.). Where?

MRS WHITTLE (*holding up her handbag*). Here. I didn't want any upset at *my* house. If my husband got to hear of this business, he'd shoot both you *and* Henry. Not that I would object to that—but I loathe dressing in black.

(*She exits up the stairs.*)

CHARLEY (*moving towards the archway; wiping his forehead*). Phew!

(BERYL *enters through the archway.*)

BERYL (*standing* R. *of the arch*). A lady to see you, sir.

CHARLEY. No damn fear! (*He turns and makes for the door up* L.)

(ANGEL *enters through the archway. She wears a small attractive hat without her music-hall wig.*)

ANGEL. Hello, Charley!

(BERYL *exits through the archway.*)

CHARLEY (*stopping and turning*). Angel! What are *you* doing here?

ANGEL. I promised to meet Mendoza—has he arrived?

CHARLEY. No. (*He crosses to* L. *of* ANGEL.) For the love of Pete, get out of here. She'll go mad if she sees you.

ANGEL. Who will?

CHARLEY (*in a loud whisper*). Mrs Whittle, Henry's mother-in-law. There was a hell of a bust up this morning and his wife walked out.

ANGEL (*in a loud whisper*). Because of my lipstick?

CHARLEY (*in a loud whisper*). That and a few other things.

(HENRY *enters and comes dazedly down the stairs. He wears a lounge suit.* CHARLEY *nervously swings round. Without seeing* CHARLEY *or* ANGEL HENRY *exits up* L.)

ANGEL. What's happened to *him?*
CHARLEY. He's just had a chat with Mrs Whittle. (*He tries to persuade* ANGEL *through the archway.*) Tell Mendoza to come round later. Give me a ring in half an hour.
ANGEL. O.K. But it's going to cost you something.
CHARLEY. You mean—we've got to pay?
ANGEL (*smiling*). Mendoza doesn't work for nothing.

(MRS WHITTLE *enters and comes down the stairs.*)

CHARLEY (*angrily*). But, damn it, he caused all the trouble.
MRS WHITTLE (*as she descends*). What trouble?
CHARLEY (*hopelessly*). Now we're in it!
MRS WHITTLE (*moving down* L.C.). Who's this woman?
ANGEL. Well, er—I'm er ...
CHARLEY (*moving* ANGEL *below the table* R.C.). She's Miss L'Estrange. (*To* ANGEL. *With a feeble smile.*) This is Mrs Whittle.
ANGEL. How do you do?
CHARLEY. Miss L'Estrange is a very dear friend of mine. Very dear indeed.
MRS WHITTLE. She looks rather cheap to me.
ANGEL. How dare you!
MRS WHITTLE. What are you doing here?
ANGEL. I called to see Mr Stirling.
MRS WHITTLE. Which Mr Stirling?
ANGEL. What the hell's it got to do with you?

(CHARLEY *stays* L. *of* ANGEL.)

MRS WHITTLE (*moving* C.). If you're the woman who led Henry astray ...
CHARLEY. She's nothing to *do* with Henry. She's er—she's ...
MRS WHITTLE. She's what?
CHARLEY. She's my fiancée. We've been engaged for years.
MRS WHITTLE (*coldly*). What at?
ANGEL. Oh!
MRS WHITTLE (*to* CHARLEY). Where's your brother?
CHARLEY (*pointing to the door up* L.). In there.
MRS WHITTLE. Fetch him out.

(CHARLEY *bows and moves up* C. *With old world courtesy, he bows again as* MRS WHITTLE *watches him, then he crosses to the door up* L. MRS WHITTLE *turns to exchange a glare with* ANGEL. CHARLEY *puts his tongue out at* MRS WHITTLE'S *back, then knocks on the door up* L.)

CHARLEY (*calling*). Henry. You're wanted. (*He moves down* L.)
MRS WHITTLE (*turning and glaring at* CHARLEY). If you've been telling me a lie, God help you.

(HENRY *enters up* L. *and moves to* R. *of* CHARLEY.)

HENRY (to CHARLEY). Yes?

MRS WHITTLE (pointing to ANGEL). Have you ever seen this woman before?

(HENRY turns and looks at ANGEL. The soft music of the saw-violin is heard off for a few moments.)

HENRY. Oh! It's my Angel. (He paws the ground.)

(CHARLEY tries to stop him.)

MRS WHITTLE. I thought so! What is this woman to you?

HENRY. She's my lily among thorns. (He crosses slowly below MRS WHITTLE to L. of ANGEL.) She has ravished my heart. She has ravished my heart with one of her eyes. Always, when I see Angel, I shall want to kiss her.

(He takes the embarrassed ANGEL into his arms and kisses her on the mouth. MRS WHITTLE moves to L. of HENRY, grabs him by the shoulder and swings him round.)

MRS WHITTLE. You unfaithful humbug! I've half a mind to thrash you.

HENRY (calmly and with dignity). Upon my soul, it's Mrs Whittle. Mrs Whittle—the married man's menace.

(CHARLEY rocks with laughter and moves above the sofa to up L.C.)

Mrs Whittle, the hymn of hate, the soul of interference.

MRS WHITTLE (amazed). Are you talking to *me*?

HENRY. Reluctantly, yes. For two pins, I'd put you across my knee.

MRS WHITTLE. Oh!

CHARLEY. You'd break your leg.

HENRY (to MRS WHITTLE). How dare you march in here, without so much as by my leave? This is my home, as well as your daughter's. There's no room here for you. You're too important, too possessive—in every way there's too much of you.

MRS WHITTLE. Oh!

(CHARLEY moves up C. During the following speech, MRS WHITTLE slowly backs to L.C., and HENRY slowly follows her.)

HENRY. I remember thinking that at my wedding. I could scarcely *see* my wife for you. And how your excessive weeping insulted me. I can still see the dubious smirk with which you wished her happiness—as you deliberately crossed your fingers. If living with Florence means living with you—I'd rather live without Florence. Now! (He points to the arch.) Get out of my house—and stay out.

MRS WHITTLE (tearfully). Oh! (She collapses on to the sofa.) Oh! (She sobs unrestrainedly.)

(HENRY suddenly appears distressed and puts his hand to his forehead. CHARLEY moves down C. and looks wonderingly at him.)

HENRY (*turning to* CHARLEY; *feebly*). Did *I* say all that?
CHARLEY (*admiringly*). You certainly did.
HENRY. Oh! (*Moving to* CHARLEY.) Did she hear me?
CHARLEY. And how!

(HENRY *moans, totters up* L.C. *and exits feebly up the stairs.*)

MRS WHITTLE (*dabbing her eyes; tearfully*). Just let him wait till I tell my husband.
CHARLEY. It was only one of Henry's moods. He's been having a lot of them lately. He suddenly goes right off the deep end—then collapses like a pricked balloon.
MRS WHITTLE. You mean—his mood has passed?
CHARLEY. Completely.

(MRS WHITTLE *bull-dogs to her feet, surges to the stairs and follows after* HENRY.)

MRS WHITTLE (*calling*). Henry! Where are you? Henry, do you hear me?

(*She exits up the stairs.* ANGEL *and* CHARLEY *laugh.*)

ANGEL (*moving to* R. *of* CHARLEY). You married?

(CHARLEY *smiles knowingly and shakes his head.*)

I think Mendoza did your brother a lot of good. It seems a pity to take all that attack away from him.
CHARLEY. Damn it, we've got to get him back to normal. When's Mendoza coming?
ANGEL. Any moment now. (*She crosses below* CHARLEY *to* L.C.) What are you going to give us?
CHARLEY. Do you mean money?
ANGEL. Of course. (*She sits on the sofa,* C. *of it.*)
CHARLEY (*moving to* R. *of the sofa*). Don't you ever think of anything else?
ANGEL. Well—now and then.
CHARLEY (*sitting* R. *of* ANGEL *on the sofa and taking her hand*). But, darling, I haven't got a bean. If I had, I'd give you every penny. Don't be a gold digger, sweetheart.

(HONEY *enters through the archway. She reacts when she sees* CHARLEY *and* ANGEL, *and unseen by them, stands seething with anger in the archway.*)

ANGEL. I don't know what you're talking about. A bargain's a bargain. It's ordinary business. What do you think I live on—greasepaint?
CHARLEY. What are you asking?
ANGEL. A hundred pounds.
CHARLEY. Make it shillings.
ANGEL. I'm sorry, Charley.
CHARLEY (*pleadingly*). Be an angel.

ANGEL. No.

(CHARLEY *pecks little kisses along* ANGEL's *arm*.)

What are you doing?

CHARLEY. Trying to wheedle you.

ANGEL (*smiling*). It was rather nice.

CHARLEY. Sort of grows on you, doesn't it? (*He pecks some more kisses along* ANGEL's *arm, on to her shoulder, then kisses her on the neck*.)

ANGEL. Stop it! I like it!

HONEY (*moving down* C.). You *wicked* devil!

(CHARLEY *gasps, turns and tries to stagger to his feet.* ANGEL *rises and moves* L. CHARLEY, *in spite of his knees giving way, eventually manages to stand more or less upright*.)

So *that's* how you play golf, is it? I wonder what your handicap is?

CHARLEY (*feebly*). Honey, darling, I can explain.

HONEY. There's nothing you *couldn't* explain. Louise, Doris, Phoebe, Jenny—and heaven knows how many others. And now, I suppose, this is Blossom. (*She crosses to* ANGEL.) That's a beautiful name for *you*. God knows, you look fruity enough.

ANGEL. My name happens to be Angel.

HONEY. Well, at least you've got a sense of humour. (*She turns to* CHARLEY.) I'm through, do you hear? One hundred per cent through. (*She crosses below* CHARLEY *to the arch*.)

CHARLEY. Honey! If you leave me, I'll die. (*He moves up* C.)

HONEY (*stopping and turning*). Die! *Nothing* could kill you. You're bad for another seventy years at least. Men like you never die. They don't even fade away. You're one of nature's biological iron rations.

(*She exits hurriedly and tearfully through the archway.* CHARLEY *looks unhappily after her*.)

ANGEL. Well! She was damned insulting! But I feel sorry for the kid. (*She crosses to the arch*.) I think I'll put this right.

CHARLEY (*moving to* L. *of* ANGEL). Would you do that? Would you help me?

ANGEL. I'll try.

CHARLEY. You're an angel. Tell her I was lonely.

(ANGEL *and* CHARLEY *exit laughingly through the archway.* HENRY *enters and comes down the stairs. He looks dazed and holds his forehead. The front door is heard to slam off.* HENRY *crosses to the table* R.C. *and takes a sip from the* DOCTOR's *glass of water.* BERYL *enters and stands* R. *of the archway*.)

BERYL. Is anything wrong, sir?

HENRY (*turning and crossing to* L.C.). I can't stay here, not with Mrs Whittle.

BERYL (*moving* C.). Oh, sir!

HENRY. I've got to get right away somewhere. I think I'll go to the pictures.

BERYL. There's a Goofey at the local.

HENRY. Yes, that's what I want. Something to keep me in touch with sanity.

BERYL (*moving to* R. *of* HENRY). But what about your lunch?

HENRY. No! I couldn't eat anything. (*He crosses below* BERYL *to down* R.C.) It would choke me.

BERYL. Oh, dear!

(*The sound of the saw-violin is heard softly off for a few moments.* HENRY *stops. He looks over his shoulder at* BERYL.)

HENRY (*smiling wickedly; softly*). Beryl.

BERYL. Yes, sir?

HENRY (*moving slowly to* R. *of* BERYL; *wickedly*). Why not come to the pictures with me?

BERYL. Oh, no, sir, I couldn't.

HENRY (*wickedly*). You don't know what you can do—until you try.

BERYL. That's very true, sir, but it's not for me to accompany you—not to the pictures.

HENRY. By heaven, Beryl! I've half a notion to suggest something *much* more radical.

BERYL. Oh, no, sir. (*She pauses.*) Unless you insist.

HENRY. Have you guessed what's in my mind?

BERYL. Well, only in a roundabout way, sir.

HENRY (*putting his left arm around her*). I can see a tropical island —and the blue southern ocean.

BERYL. Do you mean abroad, sir?

HENRY. Why not? My blood is anaemic with English rain; my soul is heavy with the mediocrity of Suburbia. Can you imagine life on a coral reef? The deep lagoons and the flying fish; the coloured birds and the scented trees; and you and I, with flowers in our hair.

(BERYL *glances at the few hairs on* HENRY's *head.*)

Oh, the wild freedom of it! A loaf of bread, a flask of wine and thou!

(HENRY *and* BERYL *sit on the sofa,* HENRY R. *of her.*)

BERYL (*after a pause*). It wouldn't work, sir. You're the master, I'm only the maid. What about class?

HENRY (*emphatically*). There's no class where there's no clothes.

BERYL. Oh, Henry! Kiss me on the lips.

(HENRY *puts his lips near hers, then suddenly claps his hand to his forehead.*)

HENRY. What did you *say*, Beryl? (*He rises.*) What's come over you? (*He moves* C.) I think you're forgetting yourself.
BERYL (*rising*). You mean, you weren't serious?
HENRY. I'm *very* serious. Get back to the kitchen at once.
BERYL (*slowly walking towards* HENRY). Oh, no, you don't. Not this time. You've led me down the garden once too often. (*She swings* HENRY *around to* L. *of her.*) For nearly two days now you've been lighting fires in me, then putting them out with, "Back to the kitchen".

(HENRY *backs below the sofa.*)

(*She follows* HENRY.) Now, you can take the consequences.

(*She flings herself at* HENRY *and they collapse together on to the sofa.*)

Kiss me, Henry! Kiss me!
HENRY (*struggling and shouting*). No! No! Beryl! Stop it! Help!

(CHARLEY *enters hurriedly through the archway.*)

CHARLEY (*crossing to the sofa*). What are you doing? Henry! Leave her alone. (*He tries to drag the now screaming* BERYL *away, but also collapses on to the sofa.*)

(MRS WHITTLE *enters and comes hurriedly down the stairs. She carries her handbag.*)

MRS WHITTLE. Oh! You wicked beasts!

(CHARLEY *and* HENRY *disentangle themselves and stagger* R. HENRY's *jacket is half off and* CHARLEY's *hair is ruffled and his tie is askew.* BERYL *bursts into tears. Her white collar is off and her cap is over her eyes.*)

You should both of you be in prison. It's the only place for scoundrels like you. (*She moves forward to behind the sofa.*) What have they done to you, Beryl?
BERYL. No! (*She rises, sobbing her heart out, moves* R. *and turns towards the stairs.*)

(MRS WHITTLE *drops her handbag on to the sofa and grabs* BERYL *by the shoulders.*)

MRS WHITTLE (*shaking* BERYL). Tell me! What have they done?
BERYL. No!

(*She increases her sobbing, shakes herself loose from* MRS WHITTLE, *and hurries away upstairs.*)

CHARLEY (*crossing to* R. *of* MRS WHITTLE). Now, listen, Mrs Whittle . . .
MRS WHITTLE. Don't speak to me! You're both utterly vile and

contemptible. If any harm has come to that girl, I'll see you each get fifteen years. (*She moves to the stairs and calls.*) Beryl. Beryl.

(*She exits hurriedly up the stairs.*)

CHARLEY. Phew! (*He moves down* C.) What was that—another mood?

HENRY (*moving to* R. *of* CHARLEY). Well, yes, I started it, but Beryl wouldn't stop.

CHARLEY (*straightening his tie*). You just don't know a *thing* about women, do you?

HENRY. Not much, no. (*Frantically.*) Why doesn't Mendoza come?

CHARLEY (*crossing to* R.). He's on his way. (*He sits on the chair* R. *of the table* R.C.) But, Henry, he wants money.

HENRY (*moving to the back of the chair* L. *of the table* R.C.). I haven't got any.

CHARLEY (*feeling in his hip pocket*). Lucky for you I went to the dogs last night. (*He takes what looks like a roll of five-pound notes from his pocket.*) What about these?

HENRY (*sitting on the chair above the table* R.C.; *excitedly*). How did you get them?

CHARLEY. Looks a packet, doesn't it? It's one five-pound note rolled round fifty small sheets of paper. I got the idea from Florence. I was going to try it on somebody—why not Mendoza?

HENRY. But what if he counts it?

CHARLEY. Then, in that case, to coin a phrase, you've had it, chum.

HENRY (*suddenly; very scared*). Ssh!

CHARLEY. What's wrong?

HENRY. Mendoza! He's somewhere about. I can feel it.

(CHARLEY *and* HENRY *together turn their heads up stage.* MENDOZA *appears in the archway. He wears a light poplin jacket, a small yellow bow tie, dull green trousers and light brown shoes. He is without his hat.* HENRY *screams, rises and moves to* R. *of the sofa.* CHARLEY *reacts and rises.*)

MENDOZA (*moving* C.; *loudly and suspiciously*). Vere is my Angel?

CHARLEY (*moving below the table* R.C.). She went out to look for you.

MENDOZA. Vy?

CHARLEY. She wanted to ask you not to take money for decarbonizing Henry.

MENDOZA. Is she crazy?

CHARLEY. No. Just sorry. (*He points to* HENRY. *Pathetically.*) Look at him. That isn't worth more than ten bob, is it?

MENDOZA (*moving to* L. *of* CHARLEY). I vant plenty money. And I don't vaste my time. Vot do you offer me?

(CHARLEY *shows the roll of "notes" and lowers his voice.*)

CHARLEY. Well, er—how about this?

MENDOZA. Yes, zat looks nice. 'Ow much?

CHARLEY (*out of the corner of his mouth; in a loud whisper*). Three hundred pounds. Put it in your pocket. Don't let him see it. He said I wasn't to give you more than two pounds.

MENDOZA (*smilingly*). I onderstand. (*He takes the "notes" and puts them in his pocket.*) Sank you. (*He rubs his hands together.*) Now! Do you mind if I get to vork at vunce?

CHARLEY. Not a bit. The sooner the quicker.

MENDOZA (*moving to* R. *of* HENRY). He is so sveet! But 'e should not 'ave made me cross wiz 'im. (*To* HENRY.) Look at me.

(HENRY *half turns and looks at* MENDOZA. CHARLEY *moves to* R. *of* MENDOZA.)

Look at my eyes. (*He suddenly growls frighteningly, slaps one hand under* HENRY's *chin and the other to the nape of* HENRY's *neck.*) Listen! Nussing more vill 'appen. (*He lightly and quickly slaps* HENRY's *face several times with both hands.*) Vake up! (*He snaps his fingers.*) Everysing is goot wiz you now. No more struggles. No more fightings. Alvays now, ze respectabilities. (*Slowly.*) 'Ave you 'ear vot I say?

HENRY (*in a loud whisper*). Yes.

MENDOZA. And you onderstand?

HENRY. Yes.

MENDOZA. Goot! (*He blows lightly at* HENRY's *forehead.*)

(HENRY *seems to "come round" and smilingly blinks his eyes.*)

(*He turns to* CHARLEY, *smiles and rubs his hands.*) 'E is O.K. Let 'im sit down for two or sree minutes, and zen—no more vurry. (*He chuckles.*) It is so simple.

CHARLEY. Thank you very much. (*He crosses to* HENRY *and shoves him towards the door up* L. *To* MENDOZA.) Well, *au revoir*.

MENDOZA. *Auf wiedersehn.*

CHARLEY. *Gutten tag.*

MENDOZA. *Danke.*

CHARLEY. *Arrivederla.*

MENDOZA. *Do widzenia.*

CHARLEY. I'll be seeing you, too.

(*He suddenly turns, and rushes himself and* HENRY *into the room up* L., *slamming the door behind them.* MENDOZA *chuckles, moves to the arch, then stops suddenly, turns and looks doubtfully at the door up* L. *He slaps his hand against his pocket, then slowly takes out the "notes" and looks at them. With a frightening growl he glares towards the door up* L. *Suddenly he stops dead and stares at* MRS WHITTLE's *handbag on the sofa. He moves to it, opens it with one hand, and takes out the roll of notes. He chuckles as his other hand delicately drops* CHARLEY's "notes" into the bag. He closes it and replaces it on the sofa. He smilingly puts the notes in his pocket, "dusts his beard" towards the door up L., and strides out through the archway with a heavy melodramatic chuckle. The door up L. opens and CHARLEY cautiously peeps out.)

(*Over his shoulder.*) O.K. (*He comes into the room.*)

(HENRY *follows him cautiously and closes the door behind him.*)

Ssh! Just a minute. (*He tiptoes to the arch and looks off* L.) All clear. (*He laughs and moves down* R.C.) He doesn't know what he's got in his pocket.

HENRY (*moving down* C.). There'll be the devil to pay when he does find out. You shouldn't have done it.

JACKSON (*off; calling angrily*). Stirling. Stirling.

(HENRY *swings round.* JACKSON *storms in through the archway.*)

(*He sees* HENRY.) You Pecksniffian Judas!

(HENRY *backs away* L.)

(*He follows down stage to* R. *of* HENRY.) You treacherous mockery of loyalty! What have you done to me? What have you done to Montague Billing? I handed him that envelope—just as you gave it to me. Two minutes later he collapsed. I had to take him to a doctor. Three injections of strychnine before he could even speak. You've ruined me. I'm finished. Absolutely, irrevocably finished!

HENRY. I'm sorry, sir.

JACKSON (*frantically*). Where's that money?

HENRY. My wife has it, sir.

CHARLEY (*moving* C.). No, no! Mrs Whittle's got it.

(JACKSON *glares at* CHARLEY.)

HENRY. But Florence took it away with her.

(JACKSON *glares at* HENRY.)

CHARLEY. And her mother brought it back.

JACKSON. Oh, my God! (*He tries to loosen his collar.*) Give me a whisky. Give me a large double treble Scotch whisky.

HENRY. Ought you to have it, sir?

JACKSON (*seeing the decanter on the table down* L.). Get out of the way. (*He pushes* HENRY *aside, crosses down* L. *and pours himself a drink from the decanter.*)

CHARLEY (*to* HENRY). That isn't Scotch!

HENRY (*moving to* L. *of* CHARLEY). What is it—Irish?

CHARLEY. No. I think it's Welsh.

(JACKSON *swallows the drink in one gulp and shudders violently.*)

JACKSON (*pouring another huge one*). I'm going to have some more.

CHARLEY. It's deliberate suicide.

(JACKSON *drains the glass and again shudders violently.*)

JACKSON. Ahhh! That's better. In a worried sort of way, I'm beginning not to care.

CHARLEY. It must be mind over matter.

JACKSON (*putting the empty glass on the table*). It's quite extraordinary. In a cold sober sort of way, I feel absolutely pickled. (*He laughs hysterically.*) Sandwiches and parsley. And fifty sheets of paper. As though the pound hadn't been sufficiently devalued already.

CHARLEY. If you want the truth, Mr Jackson, when Henry half-inched that three hundred quid, he was suffering from hypnotic hypnosis.

JACKSON (*angrily*). Are you trying to tell me that hypnotism can make a person act against his inclinations? Stirling couldn't have taken that money if he hadn't wanted to take it.

HENRY. I didn't *know* I'd taken it.

JACKSON. Silence!

HENRY. I'm not a thief, sir.

JACKSON (*moving to* HENRY). Nor am I. But we've all got rudimentary tails, and with opportunity knocking and the wind blowing in the wrong direction, there's no knowing which way the cat will jump.

CHARLEY. But he hasn't got a cat.

(JACKSON *grabs his forehead, makes an inarticulate noise and sits on the sofa.*)

JACKSON (*with a break in his voice*). I stayed in that office with Billing—and watched him open that envelope. (*Looking up wildly.*) There must be something the matter with me. There must be something the matter with *him*. He started to count those pieces of paper—and I sat there watching him. He actually counted up to three before I realized they weren't five-pound notes.

CHARLEY. And what *made* you realize it, sir?

JACKSON (*his face twisting at the memory of it*). I suddenly saw a little notice—"This package is about to run out". (*He sinks his face into his hands.*)

(CHARLEY *muffles a laugh and moves away* R.)

HENRY (*hopelessly*). I just don't know what to say, sir. I don't even know how to say it.

JACKSON. It doesn't matter. Nothing matters now. I'm through. I've been on the edge of a nervous breakdown for months. This is the end. (*He rises, crosses below* HENRY *to the chair* L. *of the table* R.C. *and sits.*) I've got to get away somewhere. Somewhere by the sea—somewhere where everything's calm and quiet. If anything else goes wrong, I shall have a stroke.

CHARLEY. Why not stay with Henry for a day or two, sir? You couldn't find a quieter place than this.

(*A loud scream is heard off upstairs.* HENRY *moves up stage.*)

Sc. 2]   WILL ANY GENTLEMAN?   57

JACKSON (*starting violently*). What was that?
CHARLEY. Something's bitten Mrs Whittle.

(MRS WHITTLE *enters and comes hurriedly down the stairs.*)

MRS WHITTLE (*as she descends; frantically*). Where's my handbag? Somebody's taken it. I had it with me upstairs.
HENRY. No, you didn't. (*He points to the sofa.*) You left it on the sofa.

(MRS WHITTLE *moves above the sofa, leans over the back of it and picks up her handbag.*)

MRS WHITTLE. There was three hundred pounds in it. (*She opens the bag and glances in it.*) Oh, thank heaven! (*She takes out the bundle of "notes".*) I quite expected to find your brother had stolen it.
HENRY (*pompously*). That money belongs to Mr Jackson. Will you hand it over, please?

(JACKSON *rises.*)

MRS WHITTLE (*beaming at* JACKSON). Oh, I'm *so* sorry! (*She moves to* R. *of the sofa.*) I didn't see you there.
JACKSON (*crossing to* R. *of* MRS WHITTLE; *hoarsely*). Give me those notes. (*He snatches the bundle of notes from* MRS WHITTLE.)
MRS WHITTLE (*indignantly*). Well, really!
JACKSON (*turning to* HENRY). And now, if you've no objection, Stirling, I'm going to count these notes myself.
HENRY. Certainly, sir.
JACKSON (*sitting on the chair* L. *of the table* R.C.). And you're going to count them *with* me.
HENRY (*sitting on the chair above the table* R.C.; *happily*). By all means.

(CHARLEY *smiles happily and sits on the chair* R. *of the table* R.C. MRS WHITTLE *crosses and stands above* JACKSON.)

JACKSON (*removing the rubber band from the notes*). Now! Are you ready?
HENRY. Yes, sir!
JACKSON (*as he turns the top note; loudly*). One.
HENRY. One.
CHARLEY. One.

JACKSON *suddenly screams.* MRS WHITTLE *screams.* HENRY *and* CHARLEY *stagger to their feet with cries of dismay and bolt through the archway.* JACKSON *goes into peals of hysterical laughter and appears to be banging his head on the table as—*

the CURTAIN *quickly falls.*

ACT III

Scene i

SCENE.—*A dressing-room at the Music-Hall. About 6.45 p.m. the same day.*

The room is a small one and is inset into the previous scene. There is a door up R.C., *which opens on stage, leading to a passage and thence to the stage of the Music-Hall which is presumed to be off* R. *There is a notice and an arrow painted on the passage wall to this effect. Below the notice stands a fire bucket. There is another door* R., *which opens off stage, leading to a washroom. There is a curtained make-up recess* L.C. *of the back wall, fitted with a dressing-table, mirror, chair, and a shelf on which there are shoes and wig boxes. The curtains should be heavy and colourful, and should be hung on rings so that they draw easily to* R. *and to* L. *Between the recess and door up* R.C. *there is a small protruding half-circular shelf about level with the top of the door, from which hang two long unobtrusively coloured thin curtains reaching to the floor. There is just room for a person to stand concealed by the curtains which draw together and meet* C. *There is a shelf up* R. *from which hang sundry feminine garments, and a similar shelf* C. *of the wall* L. *There are two costume baskets, one up* R. *and one* L. *An old armchair stands down* R. *and there is an old-fashioned couch against the wall up* L. *A worn strip of carpet covers the centre of the floor and there is a fire-bucket down* L. *Although sideways to the audience, the mirror in the make-up recess should be clouded. No light points are necessary. The shaded light bulb over the mirror is not on.*

(*See the Ground Plan and Photograph of the Scene.*)

When the CURTAIN *rises, the room is empty. The doors are closed, the recess curtains are open and the curtains up* C. *are closed. During the scene, whenever the door up* R.C. *is opened, music from the music-hall stage off, swells up and fades when the door is closed. After a few moments, the door up* R.C. *is cautiously opened and* CHARLEY *peeps into the room. He wears a hat and scarf. He moves forward and glances round, leaving the door ajar. He tiptoes to the door* R., *cautiously opens it and peers off.*

CHARLEY. Oh! (*He closes the door, turns, looks towards the recess, then moves quickly to the door up* R.C. *and speaks off in a loud whisper.*) Sss, sss! O.K. (*He moves* L.C.)

(HENRY *enters hurriedly up* R.C. *He is very nervy and apprehensive. He wears a very flat cap and an overcoat reaching to his ankles.*)

HENRY (*closing the door; in a loud whisper*). Is it all right? (*He moves* C.)

CHARLEY. Yes.
HENRY. Are you sure this is Angel's dressing-room?
CHARLEY (*irritably*). It says so on the door, doesn't it?
HENRY. But suppose somebody comes?
CHARLEY (*glancing at his wrist-watch*). Mendoza's turn isn't over for another five minutes.
HENRY (*indicating the door* R.; *nervously*). Where does that lead to?
CHARLEY. The usual small sitting-room. Now get a move on. Look for the money.
HENRY. I don't much like tampering with a woman's belongings.
CHARLEY. Don't put it like that! We're trying to find your three hundred quid, aren't we?
HENRY. But we've already searched Mendoza's dressing-room —and we don't even know for certain that he took it.
CHARLEY. Of course he took it. How else could my little packet of paper have got into Mrs Whittle's handbag? (*Irritably.*) Go on—get cracking. (*He moves into the recess.*)

(HENRY *reluctantly moves up* R. *and looks over the garments hanging in the corner. He picks up a brassiere from the basket up* R., *realizes what it is and drops it like a hot coal.*)

(CHARLEY *picks up a small box from the dressing-table and moves down* C.) Look what I've found.
HENRY (*moving* R.C.). What?
CHARLEY (*holding up the box*). False eyelashes.
HENRY. Good heavens! What a life these people lead! Nothing but deception from top to bottom. (*He walks pompously from* R.C. *to* L.)
CHARLEY. Have you seen *yourself* recently? You look like the pilot of a flying saucer.
HENRY (*removing his cap and throwing it on to the basket* L.). Well, you told me to disguise myself.
CHARLEY (*suddenly*). Listen!

(*The distant sound is heard off of the flourish of the music-hall orchestra concluding a turn, followed by the noise of applause.*)

(*Frantically.*) They've finished their act!
HENRY (*frantically*). But you said there was another five minutes.
CHARLEY. My watch must be wrong!

(HENRY *and* CHARLEY *hurry to the door up* R.C. CHARLEY *exits*. HENRY *runs back to the basket* L.)

HENRY. Wait a moment! My cap!

(*He picks up his cap, and with a panic-stricken moan, tears after* CHARLEY *slamming the door behind him. There is a second's pause, then the door* up R.C. *is flung open again and* HENRY *comes galloping back—followed by* CHARLEY, *who slams the door behind him.*)

CHARLEY. Somebody coming! Quick! Hide!

(*Distant tap music can be heard from off stage* R. HENRY *gives a panic-stricken moan, dithers for a moment, then dives behind the garments hanging* L. *The basket hides his feet and legs.* CHARLEY *dives behind the curtains up* C. ANGEL *enters up* R.C. *She wears her stage clothes and wig. She closes the door, and humming to herself, removes her wig, moves to the recess and tosses it on the shelf. She returns to* C., *removes her blouse and skirt and throws them on to the basket* L. *as* CHARLEY *cautiously peeps through the curtains.* ANGEL, *still humming to herself, picks up her dressing-gown from the chair in the recess, moves* C. *and puts it on. She smilingly takes the packet of notes from the top of her right stocking, pats the money affectionately, and places it in the left hand pocket of her dressing-gown.* CHARLEY *reacts and withdraws his head.* ANGEL *ties the belt of her dressing-gown, glances at her hands, crosses to the arm-chair, picks up a small towel from it and moves to the door* R. *She is about to open the door when she registers a sudden change of mind. She moves to the door up* R.C., *opens it, looks off into the passage to* R. *and calls.*)

ANGEL (*leaning out sideways with the left pocket of her dressing-gown uppermost*). Frank. Did you put that trunk call through for me?

(CHARLEY's *arm extends itself from the right side of the curtains and his hand delicately removes the packet of notes from* ANGEL's *pocket. A voice off* R. *is heard to mumble a reply to* ANGEL.)

(*She calls.*) Oh, heck! You must have got the wrong number.

(*She exits up* R.C., *closing the door behind her.* CHARLEY *emerges from the curtains.*)

CHARLEY (*in a loud whisper*). All clear. (*He examines the packet of notes.*)

(HENRY *disentangles himself with some difficulty from the clothes.*)

HENRY (*in a loud whisper*). What have you got there?
CHARLEY. Do you mean to say you weren't watching?
HENRY (*moving* L.C.). Certainly not.
CHARLEY. I've got the money.
HENRY (*taking the packet*). Oh, thank heaven! Where was it?
CHARLEY. In Angel's stocking.
HENRY. Oh, I say! (*He pockets the notes.*)
CHARLEY. Never mind about "Oh, I say!" Let's get to hell out of it. (*He tiptoes to the door up* R.C.)

(HENRY *follows, also tiptoeing.*)

(*He raises a warning finger, cautiously opens the door and peeps out. He immediately pulls his head back again, and closes the door, as he gasps.*) What the hell's *he* doing here?

Sc. 1]   WILL ANY GENTLEMAN?   61

HENRY. Who?
CHARLEY. That detective.
HENRY. Which detective?
CHARLEY. You know . . . (*He mumbles out of the corner of his mouth.*)
HENRY (*loudly*). Oh, no! I can't stand it.

(*He hurriedly crosses below* CHARLEY *and tears into the room* R., *closing the door behind him.* CHARLEY *makes for his previous hiding-place, changes his mind, and hurriedly tries to follow* HENRY—*but* HENRY, *safely inside the little room, has already locked the door.*)

CHARLEY (*frantically rattling the handle of the door; in a loud whisper*). Henry! Let me in! It's Charley.

(*There is a knock-knock on the door up* R.C. CHARLEY *dithers hopelessly for a moment, then bolts into the recess and draws the curtains. The knock on the door up* R.C. *is repeated, then the door opens and* MARTIN *enters. He leaves the door ajar.*)

MARTIN. Anybody at home?

(*There is no reply. He hesitates, moves to the door* R., *peeps through the keyhole, and, deciding that the room is unoccupied, moves up* R.C., *glances behind the curtains up* C., *then exits.* HENRY *enters* R., *and steals out of the door up* R.C. *He re-enters immediately, slams the door and hides behind the curtains up* C. MARTIN *tears into the room, and without stopping tears into the little room* R. *He re-enters immediately, looking somewhat foolish. He glances around the room, then hurriedly exits up* R.C. HENRY *emerges and cautiously exits up* R.C. *He again comes tearing back, and hides in the little room* R. MARTIN *comes galloping back. As he does so, the chair in the recess is knocked over.* MARTIN *stops and glares suspiciously towards the recess.*)

Hullo? (*There is no reply.*) Is that you, Angel?
CHARLEY (*opening the recess curtains and moving down* L.C.). What is it you wish?

(CHARLEY *is wearing* ANGEL'S *wig and an attractive knee-length house-coat-cum-dressing-gown. He has removed his jacket, collar and tie, and left them in the recess. His shirt neck is opened and turned in and a certain amount of chest is visible. He wears black stockings and mules. His lips are made up with lipstick and in a frightening sort of way, he looks vaguely like* ANGEL'S *ugly sister.*)

MARTIN (*moving* R.C.). Holy smoke!
CHARLEY. What's the matter?
MARTIN. It must be the footlights.
CHARLEY. How do you mean?
MARTIN. Well, looking at you from behind, I'd never believe I'd seen you from the front.
CHARLEY. It does make a difference.
MARTIN. Perhaps you've taken your make-up off, eh?

E

CHARLEY. Oh, yes—and my eyelashes.
MARTIN. Ah, that accounts for it.

(CHARLEY *turns up stage, closes the recess curtains and coyly returns to* C.)

CHARLEY. Do forgive me, but I'm in rather a hurry. Who are you—and what do you want?

(*To help the quick change at the end of the scene, the recess may now be struck, but it is essential that it is done in silence and without any movement of the curtains.*)

MARTIN. I'm Detective Inspector Martin.
CHARLEY. Oh, dear! A policeman?
MARTIN. Something like that.
CHARLEY. It isn't my car again, is it?
MARTIN. No.
CHARLEY. Wireless licence?
MARTIN. No.
CHARLEY. Dog licence?
MARTIN. No, no!
CHARLEY. Identity card, health card, ration card, insurance card, unemployment card?
MARTIN. You sound a bit behind with things.
CHARLEY. Well, it's so hard to catch up these days. I really am in a frightful hurry. What did you want to see me about? (*He crosses below* MARTIN *to the corner up* R., *stands with his back to him, and pretends to rearrange the garments.*)
MARTIN. I think you should tell Mendoza to go a bit more carefully with his act. Making people forget their names will land him into trouble one of these days. I'm seeing him with the manager in a moment, but I thought a word in your ear might act as a special precaution.
CHARLEY. Oh, yes. I'm a great influence in his life.
MARTIN. Ah, I thought so. (*He moves to* L. *of* CHARLEY.) I always try to *cherchez la femme*. (*He playfully prods* CHARLEY.) It makes things so much easier.
CHARLEY (*wagging a finger at* MARTIN). Now, now! Tinker! (*He crosses below* MARTIN *to* L.C., *reacting as he does so, as though avoiding a prod from behind.*)
MARTIN (*moving* C.). I've a lot of sympathy with you folks. Music-hall business isn't what it used to be.
CHARLEY (*turning and smiling at* MARTIN). Oh, we take the rough with the smooth. I always find that, when things look nasty, something *nice* turns up.

(MENDOZA *enters up* R.C. CHARLEY *gasps and hurriedly turns to face* L.)

MARTIN (*turning*). Ah! Mr Mendoza. I don't think I've had the pleasure of meeting you. My name is Martin.

(MENDOZA *stares coldly at* MARTIN.)

I was just coming along to your dressing-room.
MENDOZA (*moving down* R.). Vot for?
MARTIN. Oh, nothing very important. I'd just like to have a word with you—in the manager's office. Any time before the second house will do. (*He moves to the door up* R.C. *and turns.*) I liked your act—up to a point.

(*He exits up* R.C., *closing the door behind him.*)

MENDOZA (*to* CHARLEY). Vot does it mean? Vy should 'e vant to see me wiz ze manager?

(CHARLEY, *with his back to* MENDOZA, *shrugs his shoulders. The music off ceases.*)

I smell trouble somevere. (*He moves* C.) You know somsing else? My dressing-room 'as bin ransack. All ze drawers, all my close, everysing on ze floor—all my belongings cross-examined. You know vot I sink? Somebody 'as bin trying to find zat money. (*His face contorts with anger.*) Huuh! If I know 'oo it vos! I vill twist 'is face.

(CHARLEY *shakes at the knees.*)

I vill put my sums in 'is eyes. (*He moves close to* CHARLEY.) My sweet Angel! You 'ave still got ze notes qvite safe?
CHARLEY (*in a sing-song voice*). Hmm-hmm!
MENDOZA (*chuckling*). Ha, ha! Ze lovely money, in ze pretty stocking, on ze beautiful leg. (*He puts his hand on* CHARLEY's *leg.*) So nice!

(CHARLEY *slaps* MENDOZA's *hand.*)

Vot is ze matter? Vy are you so cold wiz me? Somsing is not ze same somvere. (*He puts his hands on* CHARLEY's *shoulders and turns him.*) Plis, my darling, spik to me. (*He looks at* CHARLEY.) Mein Gott! 'Ave you bin run over? (*He suddenly growls suspiciously, raises a hand and lifts* CHARLEY's *wig. With a terrifying bellow he flings the wig aside.*) So! It is *you* again!
CHARLEY (*frantically*). Mr Mendoza, I can explain the whole thing.
MENDOZA (*grabbing* CHARLEY *by the shoulder; bellowing*). Scoundrel! First you give me ze double cross wiz zat paper—zen you play ze fool wiz me! Vot are you doing here, huh?
CHARLEY (*terrified*). Well, I—er—I mean, we—er—er—er . . .

(MENDOZA *hisses full into* CHARLEY's *face.*)

MENDOZA (*quietly but ominously*). I vaste no time wiz you. You are going to tell me ze troos. (*He shakes* CHARLEY.) Ze troos. (*He suddenly claps his hands to* CHARLEY's *face and thrusts his own face forward until they are almost nose to nose.*) Look at my eyes! Zey are getting bigger, huh? And suddenly you feel tired and dizzy. (*He suddenly claps one hand to under* CHARLEY's *chin and the other to the nape of* CHARLEY's *neck.*) Look at me! You are so tired. Too tired to sink 'ow to lie to me. So tired zat you vish only to tell me ze troos. (*His hands stroking* CHARLEY's *face.*) So tired. Only ze troos. (*He suddenly grabs* CHARLEY's *elbows. Loudly and harshly.*) Vy did you kom 'ere?

CHARLEY (*tearfully*). No! (*He breaks down completely.*)

MENDOZA. Oh! You cry, huh? Zat tells me somsing! I sink you vere not alvays a bad man. I sink you did not *alvays* lie, und steal, und double cross.

CHARLEY (*weeping freely*). No.

MENDOZA. You vere a goot boy vonce?

CHARLEY (*nodding and weeping*). Yes.

MENDOZA. You are going to be a goot boy *now*.

CHARLEY (*scarcely able to speak for sobbing*). Yes. Mummy always wanted me to be a good boy.

MENDOZA (*gently*). Zen tell Mummy vy you kom 'ere.

CHARLEY. To get Henry's three hundred pounds.

MENDOZA. I sought so. Und vos it you 'oo disturb my dressing-room?

CHARLEY. Yes.

MENDOZA. But you did not find ze money?

CHARLEY (*tearfully*). Yes, I did. (*He points up* C.) I hid behind there and took it from Angel's pocket.

(MENDOZA *gives a frightening growl.*)

MENDOZA (*his back to the door* R.). Und vere is it now?

CHARLEY. Henry's got it.

(*The door* R. *opens and* HENRY *cautiously peeps out.*)

MENDOZA. So! Ze little bruzzer, huh?

CHARLEY. Yes.

(HENRY *cautiously tiptoes towards the door up* R.C.)

MENDOZA. 'E 'as got ze three 'undred pounds?

CHARLEY. Yes.

MENDOZA. Und vere is 'Enry now?

CHARLEY (*pointing*). He's just behind you.

With a frightening growl MENDOZA *swings round.* HENRY *screams, and flies for his life through the door up* R.C. MENDOZA *bellows and tears out after him.* CHARLEY *vacantly staggers to and fro as—*

the CURTAIN *quickly falls.*

Scene 2

SCENE.—*The living-room of* HENRY STIRLING's *house. About 7.15 p.m. the same day.*

When the CURTAIN *rises it is a bright sunny evening. The stage is empty. The front door bangs.* HENRY *enters hurriedly through the archway. He wears his long overcoat and cap. He is very nervy. He glances around the room, tiptoes to the stairs, peeps upwards and listens. As he does so, the telephone rings, badly frightening him. He pulls himself together, hurries to the telephone and lifts the receiver.*

HENRY (*into the telephone*). Hullo? Hullo? (*He raises apprehensive eyebrows, glances at the receiver, then nervously replaces it on the rest.*) Oh, dear! What does that mean?

(*He glances around the room, then moves to the archway and exits.* BERYL *enters and comes down the stairs. She is quaintly dressed for out of doors. She crosses to the arch as* HENRY *re-enters. They come face to face in the arch and both react with a frightened gasp.*)

(*Angrily.*) Why didn't you let me know you were there? I thought I was alone.
BERYL (*moving up* C.). You will be soon.
HENRY (*moving up* R.C.). Why—what do you mean?
BERYL. I'm leaving.
HENRY (*removing his overcoat and putting it on the window seat* R.). Oh, now please, Beryl, don't start any of that nonsense. I'm too overwrought to tolerate tantrums. (*He moves up* R.C.) I'm expecting a tall dark foreign man with a beard and it's going to be a very nasty business.

(BERYL *looks very coy.*)

What's the matter?
BERYL. I've never seen you before in a cap.
HENRY (*removing his cap and tossing it on to the table* R.C.). This is no time for whimsy. (*He crosses down* L.) Where's Mrs Whittle?
BERYL (*moving down* C.). She went home at four o'clock.
HENRY. Thank heaven for that!
BERYL. She said she's never coming here again as long as she lives.
HENRY. Well, she's certainly not coming here afterwards. Has Mr Jackson phoned?
BERYL. Three times.
HENRY. What did he say?
BERYL. Nothing. He just cried.
HENRY. Oh, dear!
BERYL. Where's Mr Charley?

HENRY (*crossing to* R.). I'm afraid he's in the lap of the gods.
BERYL. Did you get the money?
HENRY. Yes. (*He takes the packet of notes from his hip pocket.*) And I want you to look after it.
BERYL. No. I'm not staying. I've packed my bag and I'm catching the seven-forty-five bus to Richmond.
HENRY (*moving* R.C.). Oh, ridiculous! You can't leave me just when I most need you. I'm in mortal danger. At any moment, I may find myself staring into the eyes of a man creeping up behind me.
BERYL. Why don't you send for the police?
HENRY. I'm not quite sure they would be on my side. (*He moves to* R. *of* BERYL *and holds out the notes.*) Please, Beryl.
BERYL. Oh, very well.
HENRY. Nobody would expect to find three hundred pounds in *your* stocking.
BERYL (*taking the notes*). I know somewhere safer than that.
HENRY. Oh, where?

(BERYL *coyly puts the notes in her bosom.*)

(*He looks dubious.*) Is that a good place?
BERYL (*wistfully*). It's been good for over thirty years.
HENRY (*moving away* R.; *embarrassed*). Yes, I suppose so. (*He turns.*) I'm sorry about what happened at lunch time. I'm afraid I wasn't myself.
BERYL. That's all right. It won't occur again. I'm going to work for Mr Charley.
HENRY (*amazed*). What?
BERYL. He suggested it this afternoon. He said he thought there would be more scope for my talents in a less restricted atmosphere.
HENRY (*moving to* R. *of* BERYL). Beryl, I'm sorry to have to tell you this but, for your own protection, I think you should know—that as far as women are concerned my brother isn't all he should be. (*Hurriedly.*) I mean, he's *more* than he should be.
BERYL (*whispering fervently*). Oh, Henry—why aren't you more like him?
HENRY (*crossing below* BERYL *to* L.). Now, now! Don't start anything.
BERYL (*moving to* HENRY). I've tried to put you out of my mind—but when I saw you just now—in your cap—my heart nearly stopped.
HENRY. Beryl! Pull yourself together.
BERYL (*moving in close to* R. *of* HENRY). No woman can forget the first romance in her life—even if it's only been romantic in a roundabout way. You've wakened thirty years of dormant love in me—and I'll never be able to get it to go to sleep again. Give me at least the satisfaction of one brief kiss on the lips.

HENRY. No, never.
BERYL. Oh, please! One little kiss—and I won't go to Charley.
HENRY (*turning to her*). Do you really mean that?
BERYL. On my unstained honour.
HENRY. Splendid! Now let's get this quite clear, Beryl. (*He indicates the sofa.*)

(BERYL *sits on the sofa.*)

(*He sits* L. *of* BERYL.) You fully realize that if I grant your request it will be nothing more than a fleeting contact—absolutely devoid of emotion and undertaken for the sole and altruistic purpose of saving you from a fate worse than death.
BERYL (*breathlessly*). Signed and sealed.
HENRY. That's settled then. (*He rises.*) And may heaven be my judge that I'm doing this for the best.

(BERYL *rises*. HENRY *straightens his jacket, his hair and his tie.* BERYL *waits.* HENRY *hesitates a moment, then leans forward to kiss* BERYL.)

BERYL (*stepping back, below the* R. *end of the sofa*). Oh, no—not casually like that. Creep up behind me and take me by surprise—like they do on the films.
HENRY. Absolutely, no!
BERYL. Oh, but you must! Ever since I first came here I've been waiting for you to do that. Please, Mr Stirling. Don't force me to go to Charley.
HENRY. Oh, very well. (*He crosses and stands above the table* R.C.) But please don't watch me. I feel absolutely ridiculous. (*He pauses. Loudly and solemnly.*) Are you ready?
BERYL (*having glanced at* HENRY). Put your cap on.
HENRY. Oh, theatrical tomfoolery!

(*He picks up his cap from the table* R.C. *and puts it on.* BERYL *turns her back to* HENRY *and closes her eyes. As though stalking a rabbit,* HENRY, *on tiptoes, creeps slowly towards* BERYL. *As he does so,* FLORENCE *and the* DOCTOR *enter together through the archway. The* DOCTOR *carries his hat and medical bag.*)

FLORENCE. Henry!

(HENRY *gasps and swings round.* BERYL, *with a frightened exclamation moves* L.)

HENRY. Oh, no! It isn't possible! Somebody must have arranged this.
FLORENCE (*moving below the table* R.C.). What were you going to do to that girl?
HENRY. Nothing of the sort. I mean, nothing at all. I was saving her from Charley.
DOCTOR (*putting his hat and case on the table* R.C.). But Charley isn't here, is he?

HENRY (*confused*). No. But he will be. I mean, he will be when he goes back to Richmond.

(*The* DOCTOR *looks sadly at* FLORENCE.)

FLORENCE (*tearfully*). Oh, Henry! My heart aches for you. But you see, dear, things can't go on like this.

HENRY. What do you mean?

DOCTOR (*moving to* R. *of* HENRY; *briskly*). Mrs Whittle has advised us that this morning you deliberately *launched* yourself at Beryl.

HENRY. Nothing of the sort. It was fifty-fifty.

DOCTOR. Mrs Whittle has also given us full details of an extremely disgraceful scene which took place between yourself and a woman called One-Eyed Angel. In addition, Mr Jackson tells me that, apart from the most extraordinary general behaviour, you have been dispensing certain pieces of paper in lieu of banknotes—and that the sum of three hundred pounds is missing.

HENRY. It isn't missing.

DOCTOR. Oh, you've found it, eh?

HENRY. Yes.

DOCTOR. Where was it?

HENRY. In Angel's stocking.

DOCTOR (*soothingly*). Yes, yes, of course. But where is it now?

HENRY (*after some hesitation*). Er—Beryl—go into the little room and get it.

BERYL. But it isn't in the little room, sir.

HENRY. I know that—but it will be if *you* go there.

BERYL. I'd rather hand it over in front of witnesses, if you don't mind. (*She turns her back, bends, and fumbles in her bosom for the notes.*)

(FLORENCE *moves to* R. *of the* DOCTOR.)

(*She turns.*) I can't find it, sir. It must have gone further than we thought.

HENRY (*angrily*). Then go into the room and shake a leg or something.

BERYL (*tearfully*). I *told* you not to give it to me.

(*She exits up* L.)

DOCTOR (*amazed*). You actually gave the maid three hundred pounds?

HENRY. Yes. But only for a certain reason.

(*The* DOCTOR *reacts and moves away above the table* R.C.)

Mendoza's after it. (*He moves to* L. *of* FLORENCE.) Oh, Florence, you don't know what a time I've had. This evening I went back to her dressing-room to get the money. That detective came along the passage and I hid in a little room. I looked through the keyhole and there was Mendoza making love to Angel. But who do you think *Angel* was? (*He pauses. Solemnly.*) Charley!

FLORENCE (*in tears*). Oh, Doctor, look after him, please.

(*She muffles her sobs with her handkerchief, crosses and exits up the stairs.*)

HENRY (*moving to the stairs and calling after* FLORENCE). Florence! What's the matter?

DOCTOR (*moving* C.; *soothingly*). Now take things calmly. Don't upset yourself.

HENRY (*moving to* L. *of the* DOCTOR). Who *are* you?

DOCTOR. I'm a doctor, Mr Stirling. Yesterday, your wife suggested that a little psychological treatment might help you.

HENRY. Thank you, I don't *need* psychological treatment.

DOCTOR. No. As a matter of fact, in your case, I don't think it would do much good. When a tree is over forty years old, I don't believe in digging at its roots to find the cause of trouble. One can only turn its leaves to the sun. (*He beams.*) And there'll be plenty of sun where you're going.

HENRY. I'm not going anywhere.

DOCTOR. Oh, yes, you are. (*As he moves above* HENRY *to the stairs.*) And you'll love it. (*As he goes up the stairs.*) Besides, you'll be home again in a year or two.

(*He exits up the stairs.*)

HENRY. Oh! Somebody help me!

(CHARLEY *enters up* R.C. *He wears his hat and scarf.*)

CHARLEY. What's the matter? (*He moves to* R. *of* HENRY.)

HENRY. Charley, Florence thinks I've gone off my head. She's with the doctor now. He says it's no good digging round my roots; he's going to turn my leaves to the sun.

CHARLEY. If at any time you find a nest of robins in your hair . . .

HENRY. This is no time for fooling! You did a terrible thing to me—telling Mendoza I was just behind him.

CHARLEY. Well, I couldn't tell a lie.

HENRY. That's something new, isn't it?

(BERYL *enters hurriedly up* L. *She carries the packet of notes.*)

BERYL (*crossing to* L. *of* HENRY). Oh, sir! I've found the money—but there's five pounds missing.

HENRY (*taking the notes*). What?

BERYL. I've counted it over and over, sir—and it only comes to two hundred and ninety-five pounds.

(CHARLEY, *looking guilty and ashamed, takes a five-pound note from his pocket and holds it out to* HENRY.)

CHARLEY. I'm sorry, Henry. I stole it.

HENRY. Oh, no!

CHARLEY. It was a mean and contemptible thing to do and I'm thoroughly ashamed of myself.

HENRY (*taking the note from* CHARLEY). Have you been drinking?

CHARLEY. No, I've gone on the wagon—I'm going to give up smoking—I'm going to give up everything. (*He crosses to* R. *of* BERYL.) You mustn't come to me at Richmond, Beryl. When I first made that suggestion I was thinking wicked thoughts. (*His voice breaks.*) I'm not a very nice man.

(*Two loud knocks are heard on the front door off.*)

HENRY (*terrified*). Mendoza! Don't let him in!

CHARLEY. You can't leave him hanging about outside.

HENRY. Charley! Please!

CHARLEY (*moving to the arch*). No, no! That wouldn't be kind.

(*The knocks off are repeated.* CHARLEY *exits through the archway.*)

HENRY. Look out, Beryl, there's going to be trouble.

BERYL. Oh, sir!

(*She exits hurriedly up the stairs.*)

HENRY (*looking at the notes*). Oh, dear! What can I do with these? (*He looks around, sees the* DOCTOR's *bag on the table,* R.C., *rushes to it, puts the notes inside and shuts it. Then he dashes to the fireplace and picks up the poker. He moves* C., *faces the arch and holds the poker aloft, ready to strike.*)

(MARTIN *enters up* R.C. *He is followed by* CHARLEY.)

MARTIN (*to* HENRY). And what are you representing—"Welcome to London"?

HENRY (*gulping and slowly lowering the poker*). I'm sorry. (*He crosses to the fireplace.*) I thought you were somebody else. (*He replaces the poker in the fireplace.*)

MARTIN (*moving down* C.; *ominously*). Yes—there's more going on here than meets the eye.

CHARLEY (*removing his hat and tossing it on the table* R.C.). You're dead right. (*He moves below the table* R.C.)

(MARTIN *stares hard at* CHARLEY *then moves to* L. *of him.* HENRY *moves down* L.)

MARTIN. Have you got a sister on the halls?

CHARLEY. No.

MARTIN. Well, that's extraordinary! I could have sworn I saw your face in a dressing-room this evening.

CHARLEY. So you did.

MARTIN. Don't talk silly! (*Briskly as he moves* L.C. *To* HENRY.) Mr Stirling, I've just called to tell you that we've found out what happened to that fellow who couldn't stop laughing.

HENRY. Oh?

MARTIN. He lodged a complaint against a certain music-hall

artist—but I don't think there's anything to it. He's recovered his memory all right.

HENRY. Good.

MARTIN (*heavily and suspiciously*). But I still can't work out why you should have nearly fainted when you heard I was a detective. (*He turns to* CHARLEY.) Have *you* any clue to that?

CHARLEY (*moving to* C.). Oh, yes, rather.

HENRY (*moving behind* MARTIN; *frantically*). No!

CHARLEY. You see, yesterday evening he took three hundred pounds from the bank.

MARTIN. Are you fooling?

CHARLEY. No. He's still got it. Haven't you, Henry?

(HENRY *holds his head and turns his back to* MARTIN.)

MARTIN. Do you mean three hundred pounds that didn't belong to him?

CHARLEY. Yes. Oh, he's been terribly worried. The manager called here twice to collect it—and what do you think we gave him? (*He whispers in* MARTIN's *ear, then laughs.*) If you knew what's been happening to that money, you'd scream.

MARTIN (*grimly*). Would I!

CHARLEY. I pinched ten quid of it last night—and another fiver this afternoon. (*He suddenly becomes serious.*) But I'm not going to do it again. It's naughty.

HENRY. Naughty!

(CHARLEY *turns away and moves above the table.* MARTIN, *angry and suspicious, follows to* L. *of him. The* DOCTOR *enters and comes hurriedly down the stairs. He has a form and a fountain-pen in his hands.*)

DOCTOR (*moving down* L.C.). Mr Stirling, I'm sorry to bother you but, as your doctor, I'm afraid I must ask for your registration number.

HENRY (*moving to* L. *of the* DOCTOR). T.C.C.T. two dash two two.

DOCTOR. Yes, yes, I'll give you something for that, but what is the number?

HENRY. That *is* it.

DOCTOR. Oh! I see. (*He shakes his fountain-pen.*) Oh, dear! No ink in my pencil. (*He turns to the stairs.*) I'll have to come back again.

MARTIN (*moving up* C.). Er—Doctor.

(CHARLEY *takes a packet of cigarettes and his lighter from his pocket and lights a cigarette.*)

DOCTOR (*stopping and turning*). Yes?

MARTIN (*indicating* HENRY). Are you looking *after* Mr Stirling?

DOCTOR. I'm doing my best.

MARTIN. Is he at all—er . . . ? (*He unobtrusively circles a finger near his temple.*)

DOCTOR. Oh, most definitely.

(CHARLEY *suddenly makes an exclamation and stubs his cigarette out.*)

CHARLEY (*smacking his own hand*). Smoking again! You naughty, naughty boy.

MARTIN (*to the* DOCTOR; *indicating* CHARLEY). And what about that one?

DOCTOR (*loudly*). Oh, good heavens, he's *quite* hopeless! I'm not wasting any more time on him. (*He goes up two stairs, then stops and turns.*) You ask him about his umbrella.

(*He exits up the stairs.* CHARLEY *moves to* MARTIN, *and brings him down* C.)

CHARLEY (*smilingly*). When he talks about my umbrella, he means my mother.

(MARTIN *nods, crosses* CHARLEY *and makes for the arch.*)

(*He stops* MARTIN.) He's a sweet old fellow—and terribly interesting. He's got two carbuncles.

MARTIN (*getting nervous*). Is that so?

CHARLEY. One's at Swiss Cottage and the other's at Victoria.

(MARTIN'S *eyes dilate and he tries to back to the arch.* CHARLEY *stops him.*)

And his mother was an octopus.

(MARTIN *makes a frightened whimpering noise that swells in volume as he suddenly and insanely waggles his arms and legs, then turns and tears off through the archway.*)

(*He moves down* C.) Well, what a rude man!

HENRY (*moving to* L. *of* CHARLEY; *frantically*). Why did you tell him about that money?

CHARLEY. I only told him the truth.

HENRY. But you've never told people the truth before. What's happened to you?

CHARLEY (*in* MENDOZA'S *voice*). I joost vant to be a goot boy.

ANGEL (*off*). Leave it to me.

MENDOZA (*off*). No! No! I do it myself.

(HENRY, *with a cry of dismay, turns and dashes up the stairs. As he disappears* MENDOZA *and* ANGEL *enter through the archway.* MENDOZA *wears his stage clothes.* ANGEL *carries her handbag.* CHARLEY *moves down* L.C.)

(*He moves down* R.C. *He claps his hands together. To* CHARLEY. *Pathetically and appealingly.*) Plis! Be nice wiz us. Zere 'as bin so much trouble in ze manager's office. Vun more complaint—und all our dates vill be cancelled. Ve will starve.

CHARLEY (*to* ANGEL). Is this true?

ANGEL (*moving down* C. *and glaring at* MENDOZA). Yes, and he's asked for it. (*She turns to* CHARLEY.) He doesn't know how to control his power. He loses his temper, ties people up and then forgets to undo them. Now somebody's complained to the police.

MENDOZA (*nearly in tears*). Plis! Tell ze little man zat I do not vant 'is money. I vish only to be 'appy wiz everybody.

CHARLEY. So like my mother.

ANGEL (*quickly; to* CHARLEY). Could you give him a drink, do you think? We've got the second house to do yet, and his nerves are shot to hell.

CHARLEY. Sure! (*To* MENDOZA.) There's some cooking sherry in the kitchen.

MENDOZA. Oh, sank you. (*He moves to the arch then turns.*) Vould zere be som food as vell?

CHARLEY. Plenty—help yourself.

MENDOZA. Zat is so sveet. Vun day, I will teach *you* 'ow to make ze passes.

(*He exits through the archway.*)

CHARLEY (*to* ANGEL). I learnt that when I was fifteen. But I'm a good boy now——

(ANGEL *smilingly moves towards* CHARLEY.)

(*He backs to* L.) —I hope.

ANGEL. Charley.

CHARLEY. Yes?

ANGEL. It was an awful disappointment—losing that lovely three hundred pounds. You wouldn't make me a little present, would you? Just to show there's no ill feeling.

CHARLEY. What sort of present?

ANGEL (*sitting on the sofa*). Well—say fifty pounds?

CHARLEY (*sitting* L. *of* ANGEL *on the sofa*). Don't be funny, darling—I haven't got a bean.

(HONEY *enters through the archway.*)

ANGEL. Oh, please, Charley. Be nice to me.

CHARLEY (*smiling*). That would be awfully easy.

ANGEL. You like me, don't you?

CHARLEY. You know I do.

ANGEL. Then kiss me.

(CHARLEY *takes* ANGEL *in his arms, and is just about to kiss her when he suddenly looks up.*)

CHARLEY. What am I doing?

ANGEL. You were going to kiss me.

CHARLEY. I know. (*Freeing himself.*) But I mustn't.

ANGEL. Why not?

CHARLEY. It's naughty.

(HONEY *looks amazed.*)

ANGEL. O.K. But it wouldn't be naughty to give me fifty pounds, would it?

CHARLEY. Of course it would. Whenever I get money, I must give it all to Honey.

HONEY (*moving down* C.). Oh, you darling!

(ANGEL *looks around and gives an irritated exclamation.* CHARLEY *rises.*)

CHARLEY (*crossing quickly to* HONEY). Hullo, my pet!

HONEY. That was the sweetest remark I've ever heard.

(CHARLEY *and* HONEY *embrace.* ANGEL *rises and moves* L. CHARLEY *suddenly looks worried and releases* HONEY.)

Is anything wrong?

CHARLEY. Yes. I think you ought to make an honest man of me.

HONEY. Oh, darling, what do you mean?

CHARLEY. I think we ought to get married.

HONEY. Are you fooling?

CHARLEY. It doesn't sound a bit like me, does it? But I think we should.

HONEY. Could I have a little mink instead of a wedding cake?

CHARLEY. I'll have to form a company.

HONEY (*suddenly*). Oh, darling, give me ten shillings, I haven't paid the taxi.

CHARLEY (*taking a five-pound note from his pocket*). Do you mean to say you haven't any money? Oh, my sweet—(*he hands* HONEY *the note*) here's a fiver.

HONEY. Thank you, darling.

(*She exits through the archway.* CHARLEY *moves* R.C. HENRY, *the* DOCTOR *and* BERYL *enter and come down the stairs.*)

HENRY (*as he descends*). Charley! This is getting serious. The doctor wants to take me away. (*He hurries to* CHARLEY.)

CHARLEY (*moving protectingly between* HENRY *and the* DOCTOR). Over my dead body. (*To the* DOCTOR.) You can't do this to him. (*To* ANGEL.) Tell the old fool what happened.

(*The* DOCTOR *stands up* C. BERYL *remains on the stairs.*)

ANGEL. He was hypnotized last Thursday and brought back to normal today. If you don't believe that that accounts for everything—(*she hands a visiting card to the* DOCTOR) *you* come up and see us some time.

DOCTOR (*glancing at the card*). You mean to say I've been wasting my time again?

CHARLEY. You've been a proper nuisance.

DOCTOR (*tearing the card into pieces*). Oh, damn and damnation! And I've Mrs Elvin to see to yet. She gave birth to eight and a half pounds this morning—her husband's ill and there's nobody to look after it. (*He moves to the table* R.C.)

BERYL (*crossing to* L. *of the* DOCTOR). Oh, Doctor, could I?

DOCTOR (*surprised*). Do you mean that, Beryl?

BERYL. A baby? (*She claps her hands.*) Oh, I'd love to.

DOCTOR (*clapping his hands*). Good, good! (*He picks up his hat, case and stethoscope.*) Now don't get excited. (*As he moves to the arch.*) I haven't had a baby for years.

(*The* DOCTOR *and* BERYL *exit through the archway.*)

CHARLEY. Feeling better, Henry?

HENRY. Yes, in a roundabout way, but I do wish I could make Florence believe me.

ANGEL (*moving to the stairs*). Perhaps I can do that.

HENRY. Oh, would you, Angel?

ANGEL. I'll do my best. (*As she hurries up the stairs.*) Is this worth a fiver, Charley?

CHARLEY. I'll see what I can do.

(ANGEL *exits up the stairs.*)

Lend me a couple of quid, Henry.

HENRY (*moving below* CHARLEY *to* C.). I'm sorry, I can't. (*He puts his hand to his pocket.*) I've only got the . . . (*Suddenly.*) Oh! no! (*He slaps all his pockets, frantically.*) Where is it? Charley! I've lost it!

CHARLEY. Lost what?

HENRY. The three hundred pounds.

CHARLEY (*moving to* R. *of* HENRY). Where did you put it—where did you put it?

HENRY. I don't know. (*He turns to the sofa and frantically scatters cushions.*)

JACKSON (*off; calling*). Stirling! Stirling! Where are you?

(*He comes tearing through the archway and crosses to* HENRY.)

Billing's here! (*He grabs* HENRY *by the lapels.*) Only tell me one thing—have you got that money?

HENRY. I think so, Mr Jackson.

JACKSON. What do you mean—you *think* so?

CHARLEY. He's got it but he's lost it.

(*A high-pitched whine comes from* JACKSON.)

HENRY. I had it five minutes ago. It's only a matter of finding it.

(JACKSON'S *whine bursts into awful hysterical laughter, as he wrings his hands, crosses below* CHARLEY *to* R. *and presses his face to the wall.*)

BILLING (*off; calling*). Jackson! Where are you?

(CHARLEY *hurriedly crosses to* R. *of* HENRY. MONTAGUE BILLING *enters hurriedly through the archway. He is elderly, fat and pompous. He wears old-fashioned side-whiskers, and old-fashioned wing collar and cravat, a tapestry waistcoat and old-fashioned watch chain, morning coat and trousers and spats. He carries a Northcliffe hat and the* DOCTOR'S *bag and stethoscope.*)

(*He waves the case.*) Some damn fool left this in the hall. I nearly broke my neck.

(HENRY *gives a cry of remembrance and relief, and rushes to take the case.* BILLING *pulls out the chair and sits* L. *of the table* R.C.)

(*Briskly.*) Stirling. I'm wasting no more time. (*He puts his hat and the stethoscope on the table.*) Where's that three hundred pounds?
HENRY (*taking the notes from the case; triumphantly*). Here, sir!
BILLING (*suspiciously*). Jackson. What is he offering me this time?

(JACKSON *moves between* HENRY *and* BILLING *and tremblingly takes the notes from* HENRY.)

JACKSON (*hysterically*). It's money, sir. Real, beautiful money.
BILLING. Show me. (*He bends over to look at the notes.*)

(JACKSON *and* HENRY *are also bending over.*)

CHARLEY (*seeing three bald heads together*). What a lovely clutch of eggs!
BILLING (*with a snap*). Look after it.
JACKSON (*moving above the table* R.C. *to* R. *of it.*). Yes, sir.
BILLING. Stirling. On Monday a full account of your activities will be placed before a meeting of directors. Not only have you set at naught the bona fides and dignity of your position, you have dragged the good name of the bank through the mud of derision and ridicule.
CHARLEY. Don't talk so daft!
BILLING (*to* CHARLEY). Would you mind leaving the room, sir?

(CHARLEY *looks at* HENRY, *shrugs his shoulders and moves towards the arch.*)

(*To* HENRY.) Mr Jackson has mentioned some doubtful nonsense about your being under certain influences. I still have to be convinced of that.

(CHARLEY *exits through the archway.*)

Should there *be* extenuating circumstances, they will, of course, be taken into consideration. In that case, I will make arrangements that, as from two weeks' time, you take over the management of our new branch in the countryside of Hertfordshire.
HENRY (*genuinely*). Oh, thank you, sir.

BILLING. You will find the premises little more than a cottage and—moving with the times, such as they are—I'm afraid you will have to combine your banking activities with a certain amount of post office work and the selling of boiled sweets. (*He turns to* JACKSON.) You, Jackson, will take over our old premises situated on the cliffs of Birling Gap, in Sussex.

JACKSON (*genuinely*). Oh, thank you, sir.

BILLING. Unfortunately your offices overlook the sea—and there is a certain amount of erosion. You must take your chance. (*He bangs the table.*) But, in each case, these arrangements are subject to your convincing me that there *were* extenuating circumstances.

HENRY. I was hypnotized, sir.

BILLING (*angrily*). Rubbish, Stirling! I don't *believe* in hypnotism.

(CHARLEY *and* MENDOZA *appear in the archway.*)

MENDOZA (*to* CHARLEY). You mean you vant me to *make* 'im believe?

CHARLEY (*smiling broadly*). That's right.

(MENDOZA *moves to* L. *of* BILLING, *smiles and taps him on the shoulder.*)

MENDOZA (*indicating the door up* L.). Would you come into the little room, please? I 'ave somsing to tell you about ze bank.

BILLING (*rising*). About the bank? (*He moves up* L.) You mean something has been happening behind my back?

MENDOZA (*following* BILLING). I vill tell you.

BILLING (*irritably*). Well, well, what is it?

(MENDOZA *and* BILLING *exit up* L.)

CHARLEY (*moving* C.). I shouldn't have suggested that; it was naughty.

(HONEY *hurries in through the archway.*)

HONEY (*moving to* R. *of* CHARLEY). I've only just remembered. What about that girl called Blossom? Have you been deceiving me, Charley?

CHARLEY. Yes, darling.

HONEY (*with relief*). I was afraid you were going to say "No". You see, I always know when you're lying.

(CHARLEY *looks bewildered, puts his arm around* HONEY *and leads her* R.C. FLORENCE *enters and hurries down the stairs. She is followed by* ANGEL.)

FLORENCE (*as she descends*). Henry, why didn't you explain all this yourself? Why didn't you tell me the truth?

HENRY. But I did.

FLORENCE (*moving to* R. *of* HENRY). You never mentioned a music-hall.

(ANGEL *stands at the foot of the stairs.*)

HENRY. Well, I was bewitched, bothered and bewildered!

(MENDOZA *enters up* L., *and crosses to up* C.)

MENDOZA. Never 'ave I 'ad such quick success. Absolutely now, he *does* believe in hypnotism.

The noise of a train whistle and puff-puff of a train is heard as BILLING *enters up* L. *He carries his trousers over his arm. He puff-puffs down* L., *across to* C. *and exits through the archway. All on the stage laugh hysterically as—*

the CURTAIN *quickly falls.*

Character costumes and wigs used in the performance of plays contained in French's Acting Edition may be obtained from Messrs CHARLES H. FOX LTD, 184 High Holborn, London, W.C.1.

FURNITURE AND PROPERTY LIST

ACT I

SCENE 1

On stage:
  Chair
Personal:
  BOYLE: programme
  HENRY: bowler hat and umbrella
  MENDOZA: handkerchief

SCENE 2

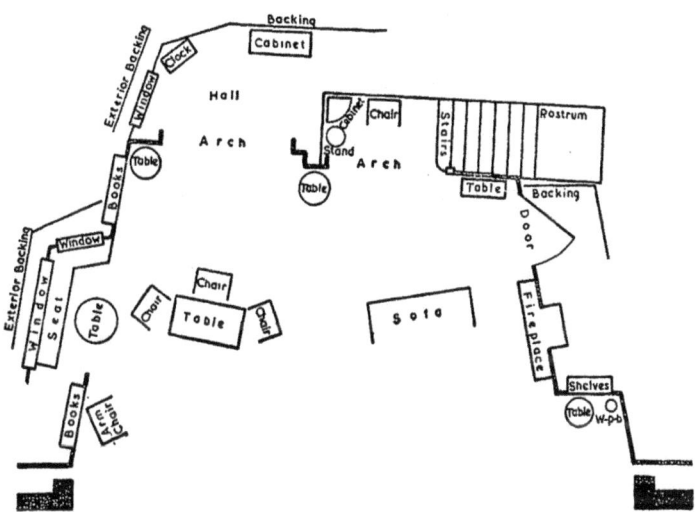

On stage:
  Armchair. *On it:* cushion
  Sofa. *On it:* cushion
  Small table with drawer. *On it:* ashtray
  Dining table. *On it:* runner, vase of flowers, ashtray
  3 chairs
  Small table up c. *On it:* telephone
  Small table below stairs

  In hall: grandfather clock
       cabinet. *On it:* vase of flowers
       ornate hanging lantern, pictures, carpet

WILL ANY GENTLEMAN?

In recess: tall stand. *On it:* aspidistra
chair, pictures, stair carpet
Built-in bookshelves. *In them:* books
Built-in shelves down L. *On them:* decorative china
Small table down L. *On it:* tray with decanter and 3 glasses.
In the decanter: cold tea
In fireplace: bowl of paper flowers
Fender
Fire-irons
Coal box
Hearth rug
On mantelpiece: clock, ornaments, pair of candlesticks, ashtray
Carpet on floor
Curtains at windows
Standard lamp
2 pairs electric-candle wall-brackets
Over mantelpiece: mirror
Window seat. *On it*: cushion

Set:
On table R.C.: medical bag

Off stage:
Suitcase, hat, umbrella, bunch of flowers (CHARLEY)
Vase (BERYL)
Despatch-case. *In it:* packet of notes (HENRY)
Parcel (BOYLE)

Personal:
DR SMITH: stethoscope, fountain-pen, notebook, watch
FLORENCE: handkerchief
HENRY: cigar, buttonhole, handkerchief
CHARLEY: handkerchief

ACT II

SCENE I

Strike:
Parcel from sofa
Broken clock
Runner, vase of flowers, ashtray from floor R.
Empty glass, clean and replace on table down L.
Despatch-case
Packet of notes
Hat from table up L.C.

Set:
On table up C.: stethoscope
On table R.C.: white cloth, tray, 3 cups and saucers, 3 dirty plates, teapot

Off stage:
  Large envelope, filled (FLORENCE)
  Packet of sandwiches (JACKSON)
  Suitcase (FLORENCE)

Personal:
  FLORENCE: handbag. *In it:* packet of notes
  BERYL: artificial flower
  CHARLEY: book, wrist-watch, theatre programme,
      wallet. *In it:* 2 £5 notes
  JACKSON: trilby hat

SCENE 2

Strike:
  Packet of sandwiches
  JACKSON's hat
Transfer stethoscope from table up c. to table R.C.
Transfer vase of flowers from table in window to table R.C.

Off stage:
  Medical bag (DOCTOR)
  Glass of water (BERYL)

Personal:
  DOCTOR: hat, spectacles
  CHARLEY: book, handkerchief, imitation roll of notes
  MRS WHITTLE: umbrella, handbag. *In it:* handkerchief, roll of
    notes

ACT III

SCENE 1

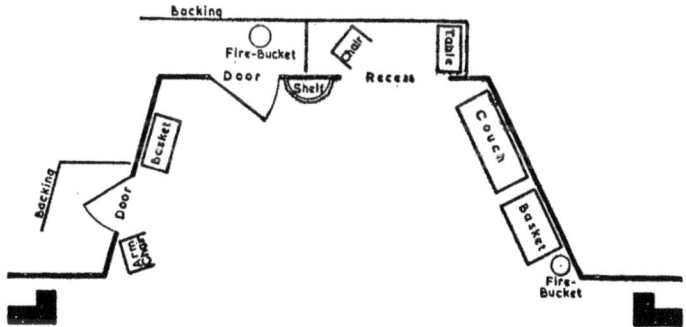

On stage:
  2 costume baskets
  Armchair. *On it:* towel

Couch
Pair of curtains on rings (recess)
In recess: chair. *On it:* ANGEL's dressing-gown
          mirror on wall over dressing-table
          mirror light
          dressing table. *On it:* make-up materials, small box
          Hanging in recess: feminine clothes for CHARLEY
          On shelf in recess: wig boxes, shoes, mules, wig for
             CHARLEY
Half circular shelf (*up* C.)
Pair of curtains for shelf
Corner shelf up R.
Hanging from corner shelf: feminine garments on hangers
Shelf L.
Hanging from shelf L.: feminine garments
2 fire buckets
Worn strip of carpet
On basket up R.: brassiere

Personal:
  CHARLEY: hat, scarf, wrist-watch
  HENRY: cap, long overcoat
  ANGEL: packet of notes

SCENE 2

Set as at end of ACT II, SCENE 2
Off stage:
  DOCTOR: medical bag
Personal:
  HENRY: cap, long overcoat, roll of notes
  BERYL: gloves
  FLORENCE: handkerchief
  CHARLEY: 2 five-pound notes, packet of cigarettes, lighter
  DOCTOR: fountain-pen, form
  ANGEL: handbag. *In it:* visiting card

WILL ANY GENTLEMAN?

A gilt-edged farce—*Punch*

Sylvaine has hit a new note in fun. It will make any gentleman—or lady—curl up with merriment—*Daily Mail*

The evening was hilarious. This joyous farce will keep its audiences laugh-happy for months to come—*Daily Express*

Sylvaine has hit upon an idea without which English farce would be considerably the poorer. The results are delightful and startling—*The Times*

The biggest gale of laughter since Chaplin portrayed Monsieur Verdoux—*News Chronicle*

Just about the funniest play in London. Hare and Riscoe carry on a great tradition—*Daily Graphic*

Unflaggingly funny—*Sunday Express*

Swift production never flags in a howlingly funny evening—*Daily Herald*

I roared with laughter all through it—*News of the World*

The whole farce is very funny. I report it with my hand on my heart—*Evening Standard*

The fun never stops. One of the best things Sylvaine has done—*Evening News*

This mirthquake is farce at its ridiculous best. It is the maddest, the funniest and merriest that Sylvaine has ever written—*Sunday Dispatch*

A rollicking and hilarious farce. The diabolically apt dialogue produces a cascade of laughs—*People*

www.ingramcontent.com/pod-product-compliance
Ingram Content Group UK Ltd.
Pitfield, Milton Keynes, MK11 3LW, UK
UKHW021844210426
5322IPUK00022B/464